THE *Heartfelt* MEDIUM

My Dearest Friend Jill!
I am so honored to call you friend!
You are an amazing light worker.
Truly talented & Gifted!

MATT 5:16
Psalm 139:14

Love and Blessings!
Rachelle B Gehman
6-5-2021

GUIDE TO *Developing* YOUR *Mediumship Naturally*

RACHELLE GEHMAN

outskirts press

Outskirts Press, Inc.
http://www.outskirtspress.com

ISBN: 978-1-9772-2568-9

Library of Congress Control Number: 2020908063

Outskirts Press and the "OP" logo are trademarks belonging to Outskirts Press, Inc.

PRINTED IN THE UNITED STATES OF AMERICA

Table of Contents

Special Thanks

I dedicate this book to my loving aunt, Reverend B. Anne Gehman, who saw my ability at a very young age and helped me understand my spiritual gifts. She was an amazing medium and a very gifted physical medium.

I give thanks to Reverend Tim Brainard, who helped give clarity to many aspects of my mediumship. I appreciate his commitment to spirit, his mentorship, and his wise counsel. He gave me the courage to listen to spirit and expand my awareness and helped me fully realize my life purpose.

I give thanks to my family, my husband Raul, my son Cameron, and my brother John who supported me with their encouragement to fully step into and embrace my mediumship. I couldn't have done this without their loyalty, commitment, and unwavering support.

I also thank my parents, the late John and Beverly Gehman, who supported me growing up and provided guidance in spirit. All the aforementioned gave me the freedom to expand my mediumship and allow me to be of service to others.

FOREWORD

Why I Am Writing This Book

Growing up, I naturally was a psychic medium, and I had no idea that I was connected to spirit until someone explained it to me. Once I realized that mediumship was natural for all of us, I had an "aha moment." I couldn't be the only one out there who was not fully understanding spirit communication and how to make this connection. If this is so natural to our existence, how do I truly know if I am connected to spirit? After discovering how spirit communicates with us, I felt compelled to teach mediumship, to help others develop their own natural pathway. I asked myself, "Why is this such a secret, when it can help all of humanity to learn their own spiritual language and have insights into their lives naturally?"

I have found that many mediums who have learned and mastered their connection set themselves up as gurus in the eyes of their clients, claiming to be gifted or somewhat unique. But we all have this ability to connect and receive information. We just need to learn the natural language of spirit, and how they uniquely speak to us. I felt compelled to dig deeper and explain this natural pathway within us. With guidance from spirit, I became passionate about how to demystify psychic mediumship and empower people to establish their own relationship with spirit. The more mediums we have, the better, as we can reach all of humanity for healing, upliftment, guidance, and reassurance. We are in a time where we are being bombarded with information coming at us from many directions, and there are so many people suffering from PTSD and anxiety, and contemplating suicide. They see no path forward, and all of this is so against our natural state of being. Many experts are working diligently on finding solutions to these issues. From medications that impact the neural pathways in the brain, to analytical techniques to rewire the brain, experts are looking for ways to make a positive impact on the brain chemistry. This might be a temporary path, but I believe the true sustainable path is the pathway to spirit, where wholeness exists for eternity.

After teaching hundreds of students this concept of the natural pathway to mediumship and helping them develop their own spirit language with great success, I had to take this to a broader audience. I want everyone to know that they are psychic, and we are all born with this naturally. Not only will this book help you develop your own spiritual language, but it is my hope that you learn to integrate the spiritual world with the physical world and see how it is all one world. The two worlds are NOT mutually exclusive.

The second reason for writing this book is to honor my aunt's lifelong work. The Reverend B. Anne Gehman was one of the most gracious and kindest persons I have ever met. To describe her innocence, independence, and trust in spirit transcends all understanding. There are no words to describe the essence of her being, as it was pure, and everyone loved being in her presence. She was truly an amazing medium, revered all over the world. The Gehman family traditionally have always naturally discussed and pondered deep concepts of philosophy and world religion, including the spirit world and its construct. We pondered the laws of physics, universal principles, philosophy, psychology, and world religions. When my aunt stepped into her mediumship gifts at the age of fourteen, she was the youngest medium to be ordained as a spiritualist minister through the National Spiritualist Association of Churches. There was always a deep love in our family and an unspoken reverence for everyone's spirit in the Gehman family, honoring and celebrating everyone's talents and uniqueness. Many spirit messages were given and shared naturally within the family. This is where my aunt learned to revere all humanity, and all people. We were taught to seek our own spiritual truth and work together to seek spiritual truth. Every member of our family came into this family with a deep desire and hunger for this connection, as well as the deep desire for personal growth, deep reflection, and introspection.

I wrote this guide to mediumship development to incorporate the teachings of spiritualism and honor these principles and provide context and a pathway to help others to understand and hear the voice of spirit. My goal is to light your path to a more meaningful purpose. There is a quote on the internet that has been floating around, about the purpose of life. The quote says, "The meaning of life is to find your gift. The purpose of life is to give it away." If you choose to "activate" this natural gift, then this guide is for you. The book is a pathway to heartfelt mediumship, first and foremost; it will demystify mediumship and will give you practical tools that can be utilized immediately to build a relationship with spirit, or take your mediumship to the next level.

I will show you the mechanics of how to connect with spirit and utilize these tools in your daily life. Whether you are a psychic, a light worker, reiki master, sound therapist, massage therapist, life coach, or any type of practitioner, learning and practicing these techniques will help your clients experience something more fulfilling, as they receive upliftment and healing from spirit. This book will help you to "tune in" to your clients and empower you to guide them, as well as empower your clients on their life journey. *The Heartfelt Medium* is a multi-level approach that can help anyone, as we break down the natural steps and show you how to connect, hold your connection, and deliver powerful messages that transform lives.

Growing up and having my personal mediumship nurtured and supported naturally in my family, I realized that people would need this type of support and wouldn't have any place where they could explore and develop this within themselves. As a result of writing this book, my goal is to create a community of people that love spirit and want to grow in their mediumship. *The Heartfelt Medium* will teach you everything that I have learned over my lifetime and break it down into digestible chunks to immediately start practicing mediumship. We will first start with the mechanics of the brain, and learn about energy, frequency, and vibration to connect. We will discuss meditation, and the importance of this to build your power to hold the connection with spirit. We will talk about symbols and literal information and utilizing your body as a barometer to feel and sense things. We will discuss the clairs, learn your dominant clair and put it all together and show you how to deliver messages in an ethical and professional manner. We will then talk about issues in mediumship, and how to manage and navigate that process. Reverend B. Anne Gehman, and *The Heartfelt Medium* are about how to develop mediumship naturally, and beautifully incorporate the trust and love of spirit, so it is reflected in your soul. And it is then reflected in everything you do in your daily life, so you experience true peace and joy with your entire being.

Reverend B. Anne Gehman was a wonderful teacher and healer, and has retired from her duties as a minister, teacher, and psychic medium. Everyone that knows her or has the privilege to meet her, experiences the essence of her being. She would describe spiritual concepts from a place of love so everyone could understand and experience the love of spirit. It would be difficult to be in her presence and not feel the love of spirit all around you.

This is what makes *The Heartfelt Medium* so unique and natural. It is not about just learning one technique, but exploring all the ways spirit communicates, and find what resonates with you to develop your spirit language. It's about allowing yourself to feel and experience the essence of your spirit and your uniqueness. I want to empower you to develop not only your mediumship skills but also develop the purest essence of your being. You will develop a complete understanding of mediumship, as you deliver the best and the wholeness of yourself to your clients.

To be a great medium, there are so many things we must incorporate. Learning how spirit speaks to us is one component. Learning to deliver messages with the love that spirit intended is another component. Working on ourselves for self-development, and continually learning and growing, to fill our minds with thoughts of universal consciousness and psychology is important to be able help clients. Meditating is essential to build the essence inside, around, and outside of our bodies.

We also must learn how to articulate feelings and emotions, and describe things that spirit is giving to each of us. Think about how it will feel to learn your own spirit language and become a translator for spirit, and a great medium.

In this book, I will present all the various ways in which mediums work, so you can develop what resonates with you. No two mediums work the same. Many books have been written on mediumship, but authors tend to share only what works for them. I want to share with you all the ways in which spirit will work with you to get a message through. I strongly recommend and encourage you to practice these different ways to find your own uniqueness. You will also learn the art of delivering messages with the highest morals and ethics, to ensure your client has an amazing experience.

Please realize that you can't just read this book and be a medium overnight. Just like reading a book on how to drive a car, you can't just read a book, and then hop in the driver's seat and drive. It takes practice. But before you know it, you will be steering with your knee and eating a hamburger and driving down the road. My point is that it will become very natural to you.

The first section of the book will be about how to naturally connect and how spirit speaks to us. I will take you through this connection process within the brain, connecting to the universal mind or infinite intelligence. I will also share how spirit naturally sends the information and how you receive the information, and how spirit communication works. We will discuss universal law and how to work with energy, frequency and vibration, as everything in the universe moves and vibrates at different frequencies. Understanding this universal law is key to understanding the flow of energy, as this is how information flows to us from spirit. I will also share with you issues that can happen when delivering messages, and how to work through them. The other part of *The Heartfelt Medium* is really allowing the flow of spirit. Once we break down the mechanics, and start to incorporate universal and spiritual principles, and step into the wholeness of ourselves, we start to act and become spiritual beings living in a spiritual universe. My aunt modeled this beautifully, as she trusted spirit with her whole being, with everything spiritual and physical. I want to share with you the components of this, so you can step into your best self. I will also share with you some things to consider in your own spiritual development. It takes applying discipline or consistency in our lives, but it is well worth it, because it will become second nature to you and your essence will glow! Being devoted to spirit, to yourself, and having the passion to live the best life possible is being in the flow of spirit, serving spirit, and serving humanity.

In Honor of Reverend Anne Gehman

I am writing this book in loving honor of my aunt, Reverend B. Anne Gehman, who is now retired. She had the courage to become a spiritualist psychic medium/spiritual counselor/clairvoyant, and dedicate her life to advancement of Spiritualism, as a science and a religion. She went through rigorous training and devotion to fulfill her life purpose. She served as a medium for more than forty years at Lily Dale Assembly and was internationally known for her accuracy. It is because of her, that I will do this work and carry on her legacy. I honor the wonderful work she has done to serve humanity with a pure heart, with over sixty years of service. She has endless credits to her name, from forming churches and several US spiritual enlightenment centers, as well as work featured in countless documentaries. She participated in scientific studies of parapsychology at Duke and Rollins College, and facilitated the study and science of quantum physics and parapsychology. We give thanks for her work and honor her dedication to the truth of spirit and the continuity of life. We are grateful for all she has done to advance the science and the awareness of spirit and the continuation of life after "death." I am grateful for her mentorship and our time together on this earthly plane.

I write this with loving and earnest heartfelt gratitude and feel there are not enough words or gratitude to express my aunt's dedication to spirit. Her gracious and trusting nature is a living example we all strive to emulate, as she showed us grace, dignity, dedication, and professionalism above reproach. I write this book in honor of her dedication to spiritualism and helping people seek their own spiritual truth. The Rev. B. Anne Gehman provided wise counsel globally for thousands of people. She has gained international recognition for her help in solving crimes, locating missing persons, healing illnesses, and connecting family members with their loved ones in spirit. She has worked with royal families, top government agencies and officials, police departments, judges, and CEOs, as well as other individuals from all walks of life. I dedicate my life to carrying out her legacy and keeping it moving forward for all of humanity.

Introduction

My purpose in writing this book is to empower you with knowledge and tools to help you on your psychic mediumship journey. My goal is to demystify mediumship, and to empower you to develop your own divine connection to God. In that empowerment, you will develop a deep connection with your guides, and then start to learn how to communicate fully with spirit. We are all psychic and we all have the ability to connect. There is no death, and death is an illusion. We are all spiritual beings in a spiritual universe, and we are here to help each other, learn lessons and grow, and be of service to one another. I want this to be an empowering message of hope. I want everyone who reads this book to receive healing and love from spirit. My hope is that you will be able to let go of ego, self-doubt, anxiety, and negative emotions, and step into your authentic spiritual self.

The true self is made up of the conscious, subconscious, and the superconscious. Through meditation we learn to connect with our superconscious, which is one with God. Meditation allows the unfoldment of this divine connection to God, which is good and omnipresent. As we spend time in meditation, we become more aware of God during our daily lives. There are many words to describe God, and these terms are used interchangeably. You may have heard God referred to as Spirit, Higher Power, Jesus, Mother Earth, Infinite Creative

Intelligence, the Quantum Field, etc. Mostly, we think of God in terms of a presence that is pure love, peace, and provides guidance. We are all trying to learn our own spiritual truth, and we ponder the text of the Bible and other ancient manuscripts from all religions to learn about God. We learn about the essence of God through our superconscious, not through our analytical brain. When we calm the mind through the connection of our breath in meditation, we start to connect with God, which is all around us. Love is the vibration we utilize to connect, and start seeing, feeling, sensing, and knowing our path.

As you develop your mediumship skills, it is also about learning and growing into the best version of yourself. Constantly seeking spiritual truth, we read books that fill our minds with psychology and philosophy that spirit will utilize to help us be of service to humanity. Becoming a medium is a journey in and of itself, of healing, courage, love, hope, and recovery. This courageous journey is undertaken with the idea of your spiritual development will transform into helping others on their spiritual journey. I lovingly impart this knowledge to you, speaking to your soul, letting you know that spiritual answers exist and are there to enhance your life journey. This journey supplements any spiritual teachings, to help you see the spiritual truth with your "real" eyes. My prayer is that you receive a blessing by reading this book. It is my hope that you sense the pureness of my heart and know that you are light and love, and we are connected through the words of each page. I work with spirit every day in my work as a medium. In addition, I want to impart knowledge from mediums that have gone before us, and how they applied rigor, discipline, and consistency to become great instruments for spirit.

Special thanks to Reverend B. Anne Gehman, who taught thousands of students over many years. I have taken what she has taught over the years and added additional insight into mediumship. I have formalized everything in this practical guide to develop your mediumship naturally. My aunt, along with other mediums and spirit, taught me all that I know. I hope to continue her legacy by sharing this knowledge with you. The main purpose in writing this book is to have the Gehman legacy of mediumship continue, as the information is passed to future generations. My Grandfather and Grandmother Gehman visualized serving humanity and hoped all would bond together to understand the true meaning of life. Their dream was that every individual would develop an understanding of universal and spiritual truth, knowing the soul never dies, but lives for eternity.

I hope to empower you and impart knowledge regarding all the ways that spirit speaks to us. It is about learning your own spiritual language that is unique to your soul signature. When utilizing all these different pathways, spirit will show us how to use these tools, and we will learn our own spiritual language and our unique style of how we receive information. This language will be unique to you, created by you and spirit, as no two mediums work the same.

As you start your mediumship journey, you will step into the wholeness of you. You will witness that God's healing and loving energy is all around us, and you can connect and utilize this energy for your personal healing. My hope is that you will experience the love and the respect that spirit has for us, for choosing to have this earthly experience, so you then naturally step into the wholeness of YOU.

This book is a step-by-step approach to build your connection. I provide spiritual techniques, to empower, guide, and teach you everything you need to know to become a medium. However, you must also realize that you cannot just read this book and then be a medium. Just like you cannot read a book on how to drive a car, and then hop in the driver's seat and drive it for the first time. It takes practice to become proficient. I encourage you to organize spirit development circles with trusted friends. These development circles are often held in a home or at some type of community center/church. These meetings support your mediumship development--not only learning but practicing the skill of giving evidence and delivering the messages from spirit. I also encourage you find a good mentor and be a good mentor. It should be someone that facilitates spiritual growth and help you become versatile in understanding your personal mediumship and your communication with spirit.

As we venture on our spiritual journey, it is also a journey within the heart, exploring the root cause of any spiritual wounds, including healing from generational or family wounds. As mediums, this journey cannot be overlooked, as it helps us understand ourselves as well as develop compassion for humanity. Spirit is also able to utilize our life experiences to help others. Once you understand yourself fully, and the world more fully, you begin to step into the wholeness of YOUR SOUL. This journey will help you understand your purpose and how you are loved fully by God and what that truly means. Once you understand this at the soul level, you will then be ready to be of service to others. This will be a spiritual journey of embracing your authentic self, for the purpose of understanding the true meaning of what it means to live your soul purpose.

This will be an awakening of your soul. By embracing spirit, you will experience freedom of hope, love, and healing. It's about freedom from an old mindset that holds you back from your authentic self and true purpose. It's about getting rid of expectations, resentment, anger, and seeing the world differently, through the eyes of love and understanding for all humanity. This becomes a spiritual quest, and a healing like no other, a healing of your entire being.

We will start to explore mediumship from a historical perspective and discuss how the focus should be on the philosophy, not on the phenomena, as this is not magic. It is natural. It is working with natural law, universal and spiritual principles, to integrate this gift within your life. We will explore the three components of mind, body, and spirit, to help you evolve into a fully integrated spiritual being.

My Soul Purpose

In my work as a psychic medium, I work with universal and spiritual law to help others navigate their life journey. I strive to remain humble and honored, with the highest ethics, to serve everyone seeking spirit guidance and wisdom. Through my work, I share my insights to help others, to open hearts, and gain a connection with spirit. Through honesty, integrity, and unconditional love, it is my hope to augment your path toward healing, reassurance, and finding peace and true joy.

Through working as a medium, teacher, and mentor, and conducting workshops, my work has evolved to the point where spirit has led me to empower people and demystify mediumship to help create their own connection with the divine.

If you come with an open mind and heart, you will be empowered to receive information from spirit, listen to the inner guidance, and utilize this daily for a better life. We are all on a spiritual path and seeking our own spiritual truth. Someone spiritually evolved embraces all who are learning and seeking spiritual truth and embraces every soul as we are all the same. We are humans seeking spiritual truths and meaning for our lives.

There are many self-proclaimed gurus waving banners and telling you how great their energy is, as they are now master shamans, as they read a book or recently attended a weekend retreat. Some people start reading books and then a month or two later, they are proclaiming some spiritual gift that came through because of ascension energy, and now they are spiritual gurus. A true spiritual guru empowers others. All great mediums have studied and practiced, as this takes dedication, commitment, and discipline. I hope that the information in this book completes your mediumship knowledge. But realize it still requires practice. Keep in mind that it is the "activity that creates the knowledge." It is through thousands of readings and many years of practice that spirit taught me things I am imparting to you in this book. I hope to cut down on the learning curve and to take the mystery out of mediumship, so you can start practicing your new skills. *The Heartfelt Medium* breaks down the elements of mediumship to deliver solid evidence and deliver the message with your own uniqueness and the essence of your being. Be patient with the unfoldment process. Just as nature grows a tree in its own time, it is the same with the unfoldment and development of your spiritual reality and truth. Allow it to evolve and grow. Keep it simple and know that you are guided through this process by loving spirit.

I am going to give you the mechanics of this so you can logically understand the process the steps on how to connect, but it is with the creative side of your brain that connects to God and to spirit. You will move from the mechanics and process, to the development and unfoldment of the divine nature of spirit. As you practice and learn to develop your own spiritual language, you then can be of service to spirit and to humanity.

Growing up Spiritually

To share my story about growing up, I walked away from spirit for many years, to have a sense of belonging in the "real world." I left the belief system and laws of nature that I grew up with, rejecting my family values and my foundation. I became a corporate drone, totally entrenched in the rat race of earning and spending, until one day I finally came home to my true self. I finally stepped into my mediumship and my authentic self. I was born in Battle Creek, Michigan and grew up in Ann Arbor, Michigan. I am the third and youngest child, of three siblings. I was raised in a spiritual home, where philosophical and spiritual discussions were everyday occurrences.

My mother was from Galesburg, Michigan, and graduated from college in 1948 with a liberal arts degree in Theology from Drake University. She was so open minded about my aunt's work and started her own quest into her own spiritual truth by reading books on all kinds of spiritual teachings. She never baptized any of her children, as she thought that we were born out of love, not out of sin. When it came time, we would choose our own spiritual path. My father was of Mennonite descent, born in Petosky, Michigan, and the oldest son of seven children. My grandfather was shunned from the Mennonite religion when he decided to study at the university and earn a degree from Michigan State University in Horticulture and Land Surveying. Even though he was shunned, the Mennonite influence and values were prevalent in our family, and those values were honored. My father, being the oldest, embraced these by always caring for the neighbors and always lending a helping hand.

My mother and father met during the summer of 1947, when my mother was home for the summer while in college, and working at Inman's Restaurant in Battle Creek, Michigan. My mother waitressed and my father was a chef. They were married in 1948, after my mother graduated from Drake University, and they started their family in Battle Creek, Michigan, where my father sold real estate and my mother supported him in his business. I have two older brothers, ten and thirteen years older than me, respectively. When I was three, our family moved to Ann Arbor, Michigan, where I grew up in a typical middle-class neighborhood. My mother worked for the City of Ann Arbor, in Human Resources and my father opened a real estate agency. At the age of eighteen, I left for college, as I wanted to leave the state of Michigan and explore. I was accepted and attended the University of Texas at Arlington, where I graduated and remained for three years after graduation.

My aunt, Reverend B, Anne Gehman, a famous psychic medium and a spiritualist minister, became the youngest internationally recognized and registered psychic medium and ordained minister recognized by the National Spiritual Association of Churches, and dedicated her life to spiritual work and healing. Prior to moving into assisted living, she had been a registered medium at the Lily Dale Assembly, in Lily Dale, NY, and for over fifty years. She dedicated her life to the advancement of Spiritualism, spiritual enlightenment, and truth. Anne Gehman has always served and dedicated her life to serving spirit. She has been featured in many articles in her lifetime, and many documentaries, including *No One Dies in Lily Dale.* A list of her books has been provided at the back of this book, as material to explore on your path.

I officially met my aunt when I was three years old. My mother announced, "Your Aunt Bea is here!" She pulled up in the driveway and I ran out of the house to greet her. She opened the car door, and I jumped on her lap and hugged her and wouldn't stop kissing her. My mother was amazed, as she knew I had never met her before. I was so happy to see my aunt. This was the first of many phenomena that stumped my mother. I had never met my aunt before that moment. She had never seen anything like it, as I was never displayed affection for a stranger that I have never met. My mother was astounded by my behavior. She couldn't make sense that a three-year-old would bolt out of the house to see a stranger, jump on her lap and hug and kiss her like she was a long-lost friend. I remember the feeling and doing this, but I don't remember why, and I can't explain my behavior. I was so excited to see her! People who believe in past lives, would see the connection. I know that I have always felt very close to my aunt, and I can't explain it. It is an unspoken bond that no one understands.

When I was five, my aunt and my grandparents started working with me on my intuition and spiritual gifts when I would visit them at my aunt's home in Cassadaga, Florida. They made it into a game, but they were teaching me psychometry and working with colors and numbers. At a young age, I started having visions of events that were to come. It was a "way of life" in my family, and this was viewed as very natural. It wasn't weird, or strange. From the time I was a little girl, I always knew that I had an angel with me. She would sit on the edge or my bed and we would have conversations. My mother was always supportive, and they never questioned the origin of what I was seeing, sensing, or feeling. There was a great deal of trust in our family members' spiritual gifts. Whenever I would visit my aunt and family, we would always talk openly about spirit and share stories of supernatural events that occurred since we last visited. These in-depth discussions were commonplace in our family. And we had wonderful conversations at our Sunday family dinner time.

When my cousin Rhonda was born (my aunt's daughter), I had a deep connection with her. As kids, we would play with sending telepathic messages to the dog, knowing the dog was busy. Her dog, Bridgette Marie, would come running into the room. We would play with telekinesis, moving objects with our minds. We moved a nail polish bottle and a packet of Tic-Tacs across the table during our meditation together. I have always felt a strong bond with her, and a deep spiritual connection, in addition to the strong connection with my aunt.

I always used my intuition, and it served me well most of the time. When growing up, I would put my books underneath my pillow after studying for an exam, and I would dream about the test and always received exceptional grades when I practiced this before a test.

I always felt a sense of belonging with my family. We had wonderful in-depth conversations, and we all read non-fiction books—philosophy, spirituality, and inspirational books. But in my teenage years, I realized I was different from most kids my age. I wanted to fit in, but I never did. My mother encouraged me to go to college and said I would find that I had more in common with my peers during that time. My aunt wrote me a beautiful letter and encouraged me to compare myself to great minds, such as Einstein, Henry David Thoreau, Carl Jung, and Ralph Waldo Emerson. I started reading their work and understanding how they too were connected to the creative intelligence, our God Source. I knew I was unique, and when I talked to people outside of my family, they dismissed the idea that these gifts even existed.

Even though these gifts came very naturally to me, I still didn't understand this was my purpose. My dad had completed business school and pushed me toward business. My mother and father always thought I should go to college to get a good paying job, but never had the consciousness that mediumship could be utilized to serve humanity in a broader sense. My dad really didn't understand any other way to guide me, other than to get educated, get a good job, and become independent so I could support myself.

In high school, I was placed in an internship for business at a local accounting firm, where they had me stand at the copy machine all day and make copies of people's tax returns. For me, this was the most challenging experience, along with an office manager that was rude and mean to all the employees, including me. I had never been treated so badly. I was there for only a month, and I told my dad I never wanted to go into business. I could never see myself sitting in an office all day. It felt like prison. He encouraged me by telling me there are all kinds of jobs in business.

During my college years, my intuition and mediumship were very strong, but I never spoke of them. I learned this wasn't socially acceptable. But I always enjoyed visiting family, to have the freedom to discuss and ponder different spiritual topics. I went on to graduate from the college of business at the University of Texas at Arlington and started a career in sales. My dad recommended that I go into sales—that way, I didn't have to be in an office. After college, I worked as a customer service representative, installing IBM PCs in automobile dealerships, and traveled the states of Texas and Oklahoma.

Three years later, I moved back home to Michigan, where I started my sales career. It was during my sales career that I learned to articulate and explain large concepts, discuss strategy, and how to structure conversation into a natural flow. It was my sales career that eventually helped me to explain and articulate feelings, including what I am sensing. My sales career also developed a great deal of compassion toward others, deepened empathy, and gave me the skills and connection to build authentic chemistry with my clients.

My dad often spoke in clichés. He would say, "if you want to sell John Smith what John Smith buys, you have to see John Smith through John Smith's eyes." He was teaching me how to connect with and understand people through their eyes, to develop compassion and to listen. My dad taught me how to answer the phone and think of others at a very young age. He was a graduate of the Dale Carnegie class "How to Win Friends and Influence People." He encouraged me to take the class, and I opted to take the sales course offered. I became a graduate of Dale Carnegie's Sales Course in 1988. I became the sales talk champion of my twelve-week course.

I started meeting people in my life that were successful and driven in business. Pivotal people came into my life. Steve Kabanuk, an executive recruiter, was one of those pivotal people. He called me "a diamond in the rough." He taught me there were no victims, just choices, and that "life is what you make it." He also encouraged me to get involved with the Dale Carnegie Sales course, as he was a graduate, and he taught me to believe in myself. He would build self-confidence by talking to himself in the mirror, shouting positive affirmation statements, while looking himself in the eyes. He would instruct me to look into my eyes and declare affirmations. It actually worked! I became successful in my sales career, driving results for my company, and continued to succeed in sales for years to come.

I also became involved in the Unity Church of Today in Warren, Michigan. The late Jack Boland was the Unity Minister of the church at the time. I would watch him on TV, and my mother and I would always discuss the lesson for that day. He always discussed spiritual and universal principles and how to utilize them in your daily life, which was in line with our family belief system.

They had significant speakers at the church, such as Les Brown, the late Dr. Wayne Dyer, and others that talked about success and spiritual truths. I joined a mastermind group of "like-minded" people, based upon the teachings of Napoleon Hill. Jack Boland created a mastermind journal, and people were meeting all over the city, working with their mastermind partners to be accountable and manifest their dreams. The church community was uplifted, and it had such a positive momentum, utilizing spiritual principles and universal law, and applying this to their everyday life and making their dreams a reality.

Something came over me, and I started to drive toward success. I became driven. It was different than when I was younger, and I totally stepped away from my gift. I became a cog in the wheel of the "rat race" of life. I made more money than I ever thought possible, and at the same time became fearful of losing my newfound status. I got caught up in the success and the social status of driving a nice car, having a nice home, and driving sales over the finish line, all for that next commission check. I became shallow, egotistical, and measured my success by the amount of possessions I had acquired, judging others by the same measurement. I did not have enough life experience to know that this would be short lived. Business is cyclical, and I didn't understand money and spiritual principles that govern money, and how to direct the flow of this life force energy. I would revisit my spiritual upbringing only when I experienced intense anguish and I was trying to make solid decisions for my life. As I started to experience success, my soul yearned for something more. I wanted to share my success with someone and have a family. I married and had my only child, Cameron, born in 1991. Having Cameron was one of the most significant events in my life, teaching me the depth of unending love, and how love transcends all understanding. I never knew love and my capacity to love, until my son was born. Being the baby of my family, and one of the youngest, I never had been around babies. I had no idea of the challenge, yet the joyful journey that it is to experience being a parent. Cameron is the reason I wanted to become the best I could be, to take what my parents gave me, and grow, transcend, and become the best that I could be at my job, as a mother and as a human being.

In 1993, the bottom fell out of my life and I came crashing down. In a period of a few years, I ended up downsized, divorced, defeated, and realized I had become a shell of a person. My credit was ruined, and I went through the darkest period of my life. I made very little income that year, working any job that I could to make it. I had my car repossessed, as the payments crossed in the mail. Looking back, I am thankful for the experience, even though I felt the worst shame of my life. This experience helped me develop compassion for others, and to understand the road to rebuilding a life. It's not easy after experiencing the emotional trauma and the devastation. But I know there is hope, and nothing lasts forever.

With my spirit broken, and my son and all my possessions in tow, I moved back to Michigan in 1998, and found myself living as a single parent. Moving home to Michigan was a very humbling experience. My parents were supportive, as I moved back to the town to which they retired, in the Kalamazoo area in western Michigan. Coming home also meant coming back to who I was and embracing my soul, while repairing my credit and every aspect of my life. My mother was encouraging, as she told me that I was young enough to recover and build my life again. I am so grateful for this experience, just as much as they were grateful to have me back home. It was the time with my mother when we started having deep conversations again, as she read books like *Seth Speaks*, books by Wayne Dyer, books by Norman Vincent Peale, and we had wonderful conversations about what we had learned together. I re-established my deep connection with my mother and father again, along with reconnecting with spirit. Every step forward took time and healing. At first, I struggled from post-traumatic stress disorder, and was so defensive, especially with my dad. With much love and patience from my parents and from spirit, I healed slowly while being the best parent I could be for my son.

My Dad's Diagnosis

I had once again built a successful sales career over the years, but life was still not fulfilling. To help me with a fresh start, my parents gifted me $10,000 to buy a home, which was jointly owned by my mother and myself. I was raising my son and became a consumer of the greatest "stuff" to make sure my son had the best, like most Americans. I was officially again in the rat race, trying to make a living, having a nice home filled with remodeling projects, vacations, mortgage payments, and working to build a life that I could be proud of...all the while, feeling that I had signed up for the most toxic career choice ever. Sales is not easy; it is a very high-risk, high-reward career. You are entirely responsible for driving and delivering results. I realize now that no life experience is wasted, and sales was exactly where I needed to be to learn to communicate effectively. It taught me to articulate complex concepts, it taught me the value of money, and how to communicate more effectively overall. However, it was also the reason for the stress level and anxiety that I experienced daily.

I chose to stay in a sales career and was successful for thirty-two years. After growing up in a very spiritual household and with all the different supernatural experiences I had as a child, I put my spirituality on the "back burner." I went to college and got a job, so I would have a sense of belonging. I could take my rightful place in the world, so my parents wouldn't worry about me, and I had their approval.

I lived a mile away from my mother and father, and I would take the time most mornings to go have coffee with them. We would talk and share wonderful conversations over coffee. In December of 2003, my father was diagnosed with multiple myeloma. He went to doctor after doctor trying to find out what was wrong. They sent him home, saying he had allergies, and all kinds of other misdiagnoses. At the time, I was in the life sciences industry, but my parents would not share anything with me. They kept it under wraps, but I don't think the medical community fully understood this disease, and they came from a generation that "followed the doctor's orders." They didn't know enough to take an active role in his treatment or discuss any treatment options. This treatment plan would bring my dad's life to an end on May 29, 2004, when he was eighty years old. My mother never thought she would outlive my dad, as the Gehman ancestry demonstrated living into their late nineties. It was at this time that my mediumship re-appeared. My father was the first person that I was close to who passed away. I had a tremendous sense of loss. When I saw my dad in his casket at the funeral home, my knees buckled, I started wailing, and my brother caught me and held me. It was then I came to a crossroads. All these spiritual things I believed—were they real, like I had thought in the past? Was there really a God? Is there life after death, really? I knew my father had to go someday, but I never expected this, nor had I anticipated the way he passed.

As we were having my father's funeral service, I looked over and saw my dad behind the casket, scanning the crowd, checking to see who came to his funeral. It was full of neighbors and children from the neighborhood, as he was the neighborhood grandpa, and he was very pleased. I know he knew I saw him. He smiled at me. I asked myself, "did I just see that?" It was then that my dad started helping me with my grief from the other side. He wanted me to let go so he could continue his journey. I struggled, even though I had a spiritual and a mediumship upbringing. He showed me in my dreams that it was time to let go, and there would be a new life for him, and a new life for me. When I had the last dream, I woke up at peace, cried my eyes out, and washed out my heart. I had a sense of completion. He has been around me since then, but it was different, as I had to let go, and he helped me accomplish this from spirit.

Three years later, my mother passed, and that is when my mediumship flourished. I could hear her, and she helped me from the other side in every area, from closing out their estate to developing my mediumship and encouraging me to finally step into the wholeness of my soul, and finish my development as a medium.

Everything was in order with my mother's passing, but it was in these moments with my mother that I started to fully understand how spirit communicates. We started having this loving relationship and dialogue. Our relationship continued, and my relationship with my father in spirit got stronger.

I learned when I meditated that I could make a stronger connection and have full conversations with them. Everything that my aunt taught me when I was little was the way to develop and communicate with spirit. My parents helped me from spirit, with my further development and unfoldment. I was visited and encountered spirit often, in meditations and through messages, and I learned so much from spirit.

Having these experiences with my parents, along with good mentorship, I learned to trust spirit. I want to help you to trust spirit and trust what is given to you, so you can help others. With an understanding of the connection process, we can move into trusting spirit and allowing the unfoldment to occur. It is about allowing spirit to work through you. Spirit is serving humanity. Without spirit, there is nothing.

We all have an entourage of spirit guides around us. We are never alone, and they have the utmost respect for us, as we signed up for this incarnation on earth. This world is not governed by universal and spiritual law, as much as by man's law and free will. It is a place full of uncertainty and dichotomy, where we don't know what is going to happen next. The only thing we can control or manage is our reaction to what is happening at the time. In addition, we have two eyes through which we see this outer world, and we are taught to judge that what we see is either good or bad.

But if we start to look behind the curtain, within ourselves, with our "real eyes," our spiritual eyes, we see the limitlessness of this expansive universe, and start to learn and know that there is a whole world to explore beyond our two eyes. When we close our eyes and shut the door on the earthly things, and dive into the limitlessness of our soul, we experience the infinite creative intelligence called God, or spirit. We learn to understand that we are all connected, whether we are incarnate or whether we are in spirit. We are connected to the animals and to the plant kingdom that is self-producing, that gives and supports life. Whether we connect with the mother earth energy, or the energy of spirit, it is healing, loving, and nurtures our souls. Everything we need exists within it.

In the next chapter, I will start at the understanding of the brain and the mind, explaining how this is important when we are doing spiritual work, and how to make your connection with your mind. This mind is where it begins. So, let's begin. Stick with it, and read through it, but don't get hung up on parts you don't understand. It will come. Allow and know that spirit is with you and will be with you on this spiritual journey.

CHAPTER 1

The Brain Versus the Mind

To understand how spirit communicates, it is important to understand the different parts of the brain and how the different parts of this organ are utilized for bodily function and balance, creativity, processing information and connecting with spirit. For the purposes of this discussion, we will be focusing on normal brain function. As we come to understand the brain at a high level, you will know how to connect with spirit, and you will recognize that you are connected. Every medium works differently and has their own uniqueness in how they work with spirit. Understanding how the brain works will help you be able to access the parts of your brain to connect with spirit and understand your unique spirit language. It takes energy, frequency, and vibration to connect.

The brain is an organ in the body that is core to our bodily functions. It helps us process information we receive from the outer world, and it is made up of different lobes that are responsible for controlling and processing information, along with maintaining bodily functions. The brain is made up of two hemispheres, and it is theorized that the two hemispheres, each responsible for various functions and thought processing. The left side of the brain deals with problem-solving, thinking, and analyzing; it controls the muscles for motor and speech function, coordination of eye movements and image recognition, motor functions for balance, voluntary movements, and posture. The right hemisphere of the brain provides creativity and imagination, intuition, the five senses, feelings, and visualization. This theory has been challenged and probably oversimplified, but it does help us when we are learning to connect with spirit. Spirit communicates with us mentally through our thoughts. We want to keep our logical rational thinking out of the way when we are connected to spirit. Spirit communicates through the intuitive creative side of our brain, with pictures and through our five senses. The left brain right/brain theory helps to understand the concept of separating logical thought from creative intelligent thought. The key to understanding this concept is to allow the information to flow freely from spirit into your mind without trying to rationalize or make sense of it.

The two hemispheres of the brain, the right and left, are broken down that we can assign different qualities, in looking at this figure below:

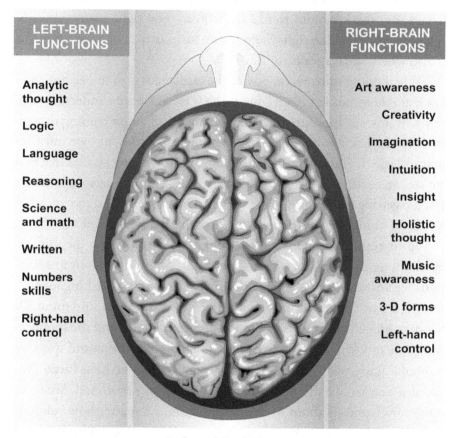

LEFT-BRAIN FUNCTIONS

Analytic thought

Logic

Language

Reasoning

Science and math

Written

Numbers skills

Right-hand control

RIGHT-BRAIN FUNCTIONS

Art awareness

Creativity

Imagination

Intuition

Insight

Holistic thought

Music awareness

3-D forms

Left-hand control

Left and Right Brain

When we look at the brain, the left is responsible for the logic thought, analysis, and linear thinking. The left brain is utilized in daily work, to process and work within processes. Left brain activity is what we are taught in school and trained by society, to predominantly utilize the left brain in our daily lives.

The right brain is utilized for creativity, imagination, connecting with our feelings, and daydreaming. We utilize this part of our brain to visualize things in the mind. The right hemisphere of the brain is utilized during meditation, and it is also used to connect with spirit. It is said that the left brain thinks in "words." The right brain thinks in "pictures." So, it is the right brain where imagination happens, but this is also where spirit speaks to us.

When doing spirit work, one of the challenges is to utilize our right brain and keep our left brain "out of the way" as we are connecting with spirit, as it is not appropriate to analyze the information coming though from spirit. The left brain is also where the ego exists, and we must remove all ego. If you enter into "thinking" about the information that you are seeing, sensing or feeling, you will start to second-guess the message you are getting from spirit. When we are doing psychic and mediumship work, we cannot allow "thought" to interrupt the flow of spirit.

Spirit communicates when the mind is neutral. When the mind is open, thoughts, words, or pictures are almost dropped into our imagination. We know when it is spirit, because the mind is not reaching for anything—it just appears, or it is almost like it was "dropped into mind." It happens quickly, as spirit is at a much higher vibration and the thoughts can come quickly. They show us pictures and associations and speak in symbols, along with giving us a visual image of something literal. We can also hear words; the words are very few, but very profound. We must train ourselves to grab on to this information, no matter how subtly it comes into the mind. We will talk more about the types of information that comes through when we connect with spirit. Realize that these are subtle flashes in your mind are from spirit, and we train the mind to grab it and hold on to it, no matter how subtle or how fast the information is delivered. We must be able to trust and allow. The communication becomes easier when we get ourselves out of the way.

There is a gland in the brain called the pineal gland. It is theorized by many in the spiritual community that this is the gland used to connect with spirit, or God, the infinite creative intelligence. See the figure below:

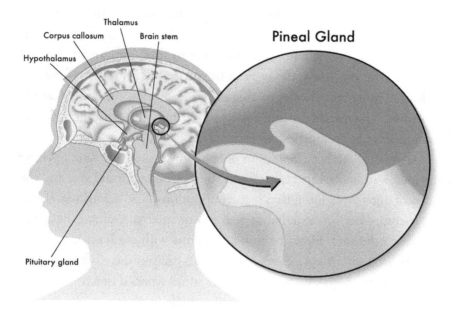

The pineal gland is bigger in children, and it shrinks as we age, by the age of twelve. Many environmental factors may affect the function of the pineal gland. It is said that fluoride crystalizes and hinders the function of pineal gland. However, I believe this can be reversed, as we practice activating our connection with spirit. The pineal gland is also referred by many as the "third eye." This is utilized to see beyond this world, have precognition and prophetic visions, and receive information from spirit.

There are energy centers within the body called chakras, and the third eye is considered one of those energy centers within the body. Connection is as easy as sending energy upward to connect with the highest vibration to your God Source, and then holding that connection while you connect to your heart. You will feel a rise in your energy. Practicing this in meditation will build your ability to make and hold the connection. We will discuss this more in the chapter on "Making the Connection with Spirit."

The Difference Between the Brain and the Mind

There is a difference between the brain and the mind. The brain is an organ in the body that regulates bodily functions, but the brain does NOT equal the mind. The mind is something more than the brain. The mind is the vehicle for consciousness to function, and the mind functions after the body falls away in the process commonly referred to as "death." Spiritualists refer to this as "going home," because death is an illusion. The mind continues as consciousness. The mind continues to function as consciousness after the body falls away.

Webster's Dictionary definition of consciousness is "the state of being conscious; awareness, especially of what is happening around you and the totality of one's thoughts, feelings, and impressions." Consciousness, therefore, encompasses our external as well as our internal reality. The mind is also with the soul. How the mind functions with mediumship is very individualized and unique. Everyone's mind is unique, therefore everyone's mediumship is unique, because everyone's mind works differently.

The body is mortal, and the soul, which is divine spirit, is connected to the universal mind and the infinite intelligence called God or spirit. We have illustrated in this figure below:

The body can be associated with consciousness, the soul can be associated with the subconscious, and divine spirit associated with the superconscious. As mediums, we want to connect with the superconscious, the divine. In the next chapter we will discuss how to make the connection and how meditation builds the power to hold the connection to spirit to receive information.

CHAPTER 2

Making the Connection with Spirit

$\mathcal{A}$s we start to discuss the connection with spirit, it would be helpful to understand energy, frequency, and vibration. If you understand the process and properties that govern the universe, the connection will be easier for you, as you understand the forces of the universe. Nikola Tesla said, "If you want to find the secrets of the universe, think in terms of energy, frequency and vibration." As a medium, we work with all three properties, and we work with them naturally. These three properties are the secret to healing, divine connection, and understanding everything that exists on this planet. I won't go into the properties from a scientific perspective, but I will explain how we use all three in mediumship.

The law of the universe states that everything in the universe moves and vibrates. Everything vibrates at one speed or another. Nothing ever rests. Everything you see around you is vibrating at one frequency or another, and so are you.

There are different levels of vibratory frequencies. Hertz (or Hz) refers to the standard unit of measurement used for measuring frequency. Since frequency is measured in cycles per second, one hertz equals one cycle per second. (techterms.com/definition/hertz)

The earth resonates at a frequency of about 8.37 Hz. The human body's resonant frequency is from roughly 62 to 68 Hz. Body mass and height does not impact the frequency. This electrical conduction creates the flow of electrical current that produces our life force. The higher the frequency, the lighter you feel in your physical body, as well as emotionally and mentally. You feel you have more clarity. By the same token, love is a vibration. Love is at the highest vibration and frequency. When we connect with spirit, we want to connect with the love vibration, which is where we become connected. I have been taught that the love frequency is at 528 Hz, which is also the vibration of the spirit world. The way we raise our vibration is to meditate. Spending time in meditation is very important, as this builds the power and energy to connect and hold the link with spirit. The vibratory frequencies also manifest in sound and color. When practicing, or when we sit in a development circle with others, many times people can see the connection of others to spirit, as you can see color around the body and the color radiates upward and away from the body.

Practice meditation daily. Meditation raises your vibration and is the power that helps you connect with spirit. It is vital for spirit connection.

Meditation

Becoming quiet in a busy world is difficult in the beginning. Everyone says, "I can't quiet my mind, as I have all these thoughts running through my mind." When you master this, you will grow to love meditation, as it is very intoxicating. When you recognize that you can achieve the feeling of the purest love in meditation, you want more of it. Therefore, you become devoted to the practice, versus looking at it as something you must do. Living from your heart and your authentic self becomes easier and is enhanced by meditation. One of the difficulties that many people have in considering meditation is that they think it is one more thing that they have to do in their lives. However, meditation is not an effort in non-doing. Connecting with God is to spend each day in that place inside ourselves in which there is deep love and peace. It is the most necessary component of our spirit work. My aunt would refer to this as attuning yourself to the highest vibration. What she meant was connecting with the infinite. This connection raises the vibration to facilitate spirit communication. When doing spirit work, you must hold the connection to spirit. The only way you learn this is by daily meditation and raising your vibration. Meditation provides the "energy" to hold the connection with spirit, so they can give us messages.

Meditation is not some physical position where your legs must be crossed, or you must sit in the lotus position. Nor is it a deep mental exercise. It is about letting go and allowing. It's about breathing and relaxing the body; as you notice and release tension in the body, you let it go by breathing through it. You start to feel your soul in your body, the operative word being "feeling." When people first start out, I have them imagine someone or something, like a dog or a cat, something that they unconditionally love, with their eyes closed. Then I ask them to feel this love in their heart. Then send this love out into the room and then start to feel the love all around you. Start to commune with this love vibration all around you. Now send that love upward out of your head and connect. Once you get the hang of the feeling of the love, you can then start by feeling that love and sending it upward, and then drop into your heart and send it out into the room. But when we first start, it must be the reverse. The reason for this is for you to feel the love. When we first start to meditate, we need to feel the love, get out of our left brain, and stop thinking. We need to feel the flow of the energy and feel the vibration of love and get comfortable with this feeling.

Meditation helps you to develop a connection with God, your higher self, and your intuitive mind, where all answers exist, and which is a place waiting for you to discover it. It is a place of limitlessness, if we just drop our ego and imperfect thoughts and vain opinions. We relax, breathe, and wait to experience the vastness of this place of love. Please consider establishing a regular practice. After about twenty-one days, it will become part of your daily routine, and you will never want to miss a day.

This type of meditation described has been utilized by the Gehman family and is the most effective form of meditation for mediumship, as it helps to connect to the highest vibration and hold the connection with spirit, to receive evidence and deliver messages. It also helps to practice "feeling" what is around you, and to start utilizing your body as a barometer for receiving evidence and information, in your spiritual service work. Practicing meditation in this way is like the fundamentals, the ABCs of Spirit Communication, as you are the interpreter or translator. To interpret the information spirit is giving you, you must be able to feel it, see it, hear it, and sense it, and be able to describe it to your recipient.

At first, you may choose to try guided meditations, binaural beats, or soft classical music. You can follow the Far Eastern tradition of focusing on breathing or something similar. Moving into working with frequency and vibration will ultimately help you develop your spiritual connection.

As long as let go of your mundane life thoughts, your ego, your identity, and all that defines you, and go within to realize you are spirit and you commune with spirit, your gifts will start to unfold. Keep your awareness on nothing other than love, and just relax. People have reported seeing white light, colors, and nothing. This is all normal. Notice if there are pictures dropped into your mind. Take time to sense and feel all that is around you.

Imagine a white light is going through the center of your body, from the soles of your feet, all the way up through the top of your head, spilling outward, shooting up and cascading over your body. You are establishing that your energy is fully aligned with Source.

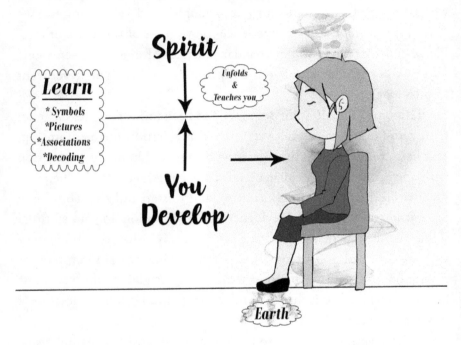

One added benefit to a regular meditation is that you won't need "things," or need energy from outside yourself, and you will stop asking for advice or looking for the physical world to fulfill your needs. They have already been fulfilled. You will feel the wholeness and not require validation from others, as you will have this from spirit.

When you meditate for an extended period, as you lengthen your time in your sessions, you will start to notice that you have been operating from your ego for most of your life. You will have a newfound sense of freedom with a regular practice of meditation.

Your ego has provided the illusion that tricks you into believing that all your desires and attainment of things will bring happiness, when in fact, these desires are really creating stress and suffering. To know your ego in this way, and to connect with your authentic self, you can totally change who you are and your interactions with yourself, with others, and how you respond to the world.

Meeting your Guides

If you have done any amount of reading or studying, you have probably heard something about your spirit guides. Everyone has guides and working with your guides in mediumship is very important—not only meeting them, but working with them, as they are the key to helping your mediumship unfold. I am going to explain the construct of your guides, as you have more than one—you have an entourage. Each guide has a specific purpose. They are the key to helping you learn to communicate with spirit. You learn, and there is an entire unfoldment that is occurring. They help change the energy, help you lift vibration, and bring forth the spirits that need to communicate with your clients. They are so important to your work. They even will help directly channel information in a trance for others to hear and experience. Your guides are part of your spiritual experience, journey, growth, and unfoldment. You must provide the willingness to drop your ego and trust them. For example, if you are confused about something in your life, and everything looks great to the human eye, but the energy around you is heavy, your gut is twisted, then this is your guide signaling this is not a good situation for you. Trust it and listen. If you are uncomfortable, then this is your guide signaling to you that this is not a good situation.

You have a wonderful opportunity to meet your guides in meditation. You have guides that have been assigned to you for all of your days on this earth. Your main guides are your protector guide and your joy guide. You also have a healer, and teachers, and guides that come in based on life situations to help us. As a medium, you have a runner or a gatekeeper, that runs to get loved ones of your clients. For example, if someone calls to set up time for a reading, or meets you randomly, your guides have set that up, and the runner helps the spirit communicator come through for their loved one. In mediumship, they play an important role, and it is vital that we develop a wonderful relationship with them. Talk to them throughout your day, like they are your best friends. I constantly have dialogue with mine, and occasionally, I put chairs in a circle and hold a staff meeting. I will show you how to set your agreements and intentions with your guides. Give them thanks for all the wonderful work they do, and they will move mountains for you.

Spirit guides communicate with us, but most people are not aware of their presence or do not understand their influence in our lives. These guides love us and have so much respect for us. They exist to help us with our lives while we are on this earth. This was decided before you came to earth, and they exist to help you. All of humanity, including everything that is living, is being elevated in wisdom and truth.

Spiritual beings, including your spirit guides, work with all of us to assist us on our life path. They help us on our life journey, for the purpose of educating and elevating all of humanity. Spirit guides help us to come to our own spiritual truth, by assisting us to free ourselves from false narratives, artificial constructs, old patterns of behavior, ideas, and beliefs. Their wise guidance provides insight, as well as confirmation, while we work to learn our life lessons. Spirit guides have a voice within us and can be recognized best through the practice of meditation. These loving spirits speak deep inside us, communicating with our soul.

We will have more than one guide in our life, for different purposes, as they come in and leave based upon the lessons we are learning. Spirit guides can also assist by helping to guide us in a certain direction. For example, when someone is at a crossroads and needs to decide as to which path to choose, spirit guides will gently nudge us but will never make the decision for us. We always have free will. They are with us to shed light upon our situations, not to live our lives for us. Yet they too learn from our choices and life experiences. All of spirit is working to grow and elevate humanity. Spirit guides were at one time human and were as human as we are, but now are in spirit. They are bound by universal and spiritual law. They have lessons to learn in their elevation, as well. Spirit guides have their own personality and uniqueness, just like all of us.

Our main guides have not incarnated with us during our lifetime. While an aunt, for example, who passed over may offer some guidance, and she is part of your soul family, she is not your actual guide. These family members and friends that have passed are known as "honorary guides."

Our main guides are assigned and have knowledge and the training to become our "spirit guide." Not just anyone can be a guide; they must have had many experiences to be designated as our guide, based upon the purpose we have chosen to fulfill on this earth.

Spirit guides remind us to focus our lives, and on spiritual truth. They do this in meditation. Once a teacher guide has fulfilled its purpose, a new teacher in spirit will come to guide us toward our next lesson. They all work together to help you.

Whether we are aware of them or not, they are guiding us. It becomes a wonderful symbiotic relationship if we choose to start recognizing their presence in our lives.

It is theorized that there are different levels of existence, multidimensional planes. Physicists have theorized of the existence of these alternate universes through the hypothesis of string theory but have not been able to prove this theory. But spiritualists and people seeking the spiritual call them planes of enlightenment. All of humanity is elevating in wisdom and truth through a collective consciousness. Therefore, any learning and growing that you do uplifts humanity forever. It is evolution at the mind consciousness level.

Spirit guides help us with our spiritual truths, help us learn our lessons, develop, and refine our mediumship, and help us serve humanity. They also assist us by helping to free us from our worldly ideas and beliefs. Trust is the key, because they will never fail to guide you in the right direction, ever. This is what is meant when Paul wrote in his letter to the Corinthians in 2 Corinthians 5:7, "Walk by faith, and not by sight." Don't trust outer circumstances; trust spirit. Spirit will never forsake you. Their wise counsel and guidance provide insight, as well as confirmation, while we work to see and learn life lessons. They cannot give us all the answers, as some of this comes down to free will, and sometimes the lesson is for you to make a decision. In this case, spirit is waiting for us to decide, so spirit can line up circumstances to support our decision. The key is allowing and being open to the way the universe and spirit responds, and trust that response—never think it is anything other than for your highest good.

Spirit guides have a voice within us and can be recognized best through the practice of meditation. These amazing and loving guides speak deep within us, communicating with our soul.

Always remember that our guides help us in our lives, but don't live our lives for us. Guides also learn from our choices and our life experiences. They also learn by guiding us in our lives.

All of spirit is working to grow and elevate the mind consciousness and humanity. When we learn, it uplifts people around us, and extends out to our family and to all of humanity. Spirit guides were once human and had human experiences. They are at the highest vibration of love. They have lessons to learn, as well, and have the utmost and deepest respect that we chose to come to this earthly plane of existence to have this physical experience to learn and grow. There are different planes of existence, but our guides are closest to the earth plane. For the purposes of this book, I am not going into the different planes of existence, as I want to stay in the confines of the development of your mediumship. However, if you are curious, there are many books on the 4th and 5th dimensions.

Some people find it easy to comprehend their guides, while others struggle to believe in their existence. Meditation is vital to build the energy which lifts the vibration to connect and hear spirit. We all hear and see spirit differently. We will talk about this in the next chapter, on the ways we receive information.

Any answer to any question we could ever imagine is in our "cell memory" in the body, as well as or "soul," and when we connect with spirit, we receive answers. It is that part of us, the energy which never dies, but only transforms when the body no longer functions. The body falls away, and we become pure spirit again. This is our soul—our pure soul, not our human self.

Construct of Your Spirit Guides

We are born with two main guides in our lives. These have been assigned and agreed to before we chose to incarnate. These chosen entities agree on the construct. You are the earthly spirit being incarnate. You have a main protector guide and a joy guide. These are teachers or messengers whom we have known before incarnating into the physical world. Our main guide is our guardian or protector, one who is with us in spirit from birth through to our physical passing. This guide most likely helps us with our life-path, providing direction, protection, and guidance, much like the belief in the existence of a guardian angel. Psalms 91:11 refers to this in the Bible, mentioning an angel that is assigned to us for all of our days.

Protector Guide

Our protector is also known as main guide or sometimes called our gate guides. This guide is with us most of the time and loves us so dearly. They are not in a position of judgment, but of love and understanding. They know all our secrets, our inner workings, and help us deal with our everyday matters. Because they are so close to us, they serve as a link to all the guides, spirits, and energies in the spirit world. They protect us, knowing what is best for us, and even guard the gate between the two worlds by helping us to balance the activities of our higher selves with those of our earthly selves.

Joy Guides

Joy guides help us to keep the joy in our lives, to remember to play, to laugh and to keep our inner child alive. We feel the presence of this guide most strongly in the moments when our spirits are unfettered, and our souls are lighthearted. They can also provide situations in our life to make us laugh and be joyful, to remind us to lighten up and enjoy life. Joy guides may also nudge us in times of great sorrow, to get us to smile. This can happen when we are somber; you may see someone just start laughing and no one understands why. I believe it is our joy guide, telling us enjoy life and to lighten up. All will be well.

Healer and Teacher Guides

These beings are our spiritual physicians and teachers. They are often of a higher vibration and are highly evolved, and sometimes have to come down from a different plane of existence. They work with us to develop our talents and to maintain our emotional, mental, and physical health. They assist us in balancing our hormonal and chemical makeup. If we are dealing with a health crisis, they will enter to help with the path of healing or guide us to the right practitioners on earth to help. They can bring forth healing messages that all will be well. They guide us to seek wisdom or inspire us to create or even help us make the right choices to heal ourselves. Unlike our protectors and joy guides, whose presence is lifelong, doctors and teachers may come and go throughout our lives, depending on the lessons and achievements.

Ascended and Universal Masters

These beings often have names that we are familiar with; many of us recognize them as figures from history. Usually these ascended masters were great spiritual teachers when they existed on this physical plane, and they continue to guide us and influence masses of people from their positions now in the spiritual realm, if we choose to listen. Jesus, Buddha, Mohammed, St. Germaine, Quan Yin, Mother Mary— all of these are ascended masters. All of them are available to us if we choose to work with them. You may think, "Why would Buddha or Jesus talk to me!? He's way too busy!" Let me assure you, we are all loved beyond that, and they can replicate themselves and are available to help anyone who just simply calls on them for help. These ascended masters are compassionate and understanding, with no judgment, and full of empathy.

Universal Masters

Universal Master guides are usually easy to recognize because their energy is much different from the energies of the other guides that are around us. They bring to us a sense of calm contentment, and sometimes it is hard to disengage from their energies simply because they are so beautiful and peaceful to experience. It can be extremely intoxicating. Universal Master guides concern themselves with teaching and guiding us on our path to enlightenment. Most of the time, our master guide corresponds to the path that feels most comfortable to us on our spiritual journey. For instance, a person who follows Christianity and feels comfortable in that religion might have the disciple Peter or another saint, like St. Germaine or Jesus, as their Master guide. These guides understand that our lives on earth are filled with mundane events, and they support us in everything we do. They send love and help whenever we need it most. However, these guides do not give messages to us about our day-to-day lives. They give comfort, love, and understanding. We will feel comfort when they are around. They never waste their words on trivial things.

Construct of your Spirit Guides

Meditation Exercise to Meet Your Guides and Practice the Love Vibration

Either remain in silence, or turn on some wonderful relaxing, soothing meditation music. Sit in a quiet place in a chair, with feet on the floor and your spine straight. Close your eyes and place your hands palms-up on your lap. Close your eyes and focus on your breath. Breathe in and breathe out. Start to imagine, as you are exhaling, that you breathe out everything that no longer serves you. If you are feeling tightness or tension in your body, release it as you exhale. Take a moment to focus on your feet and relax all of your muscles in your feet and keep breathing. Move your attention to your calves and relax your calves. Continue all the way up your body, breathing in to relax, and release any area that is tense, and breathe out any tension. When you inhale this time, imagine the energy moving all the way through your body, and up through the crown of your head, and connect with your God Source. Hold this and feel the love coming from God. Now focus your attention on the heart, and start to express love from your heart, outward into the room. If this is difficult for you, think about someone, a son or daughter, or an animal that you love unconditionally. Imagine this person in front of you and express love from your heart to this person. Now start to express love from your heart into the room. Now hold this love and start invite your guides in and feel their love for you. Start to blend with spirit. Feel spirit and feel your soul. Invite your guides in. Start to meet your guides. Ask them to step in. Ask them to show you what they look like and feel and sense their presence. Ask their names and let them know you appreciate them, and you are grateful for them. Start to have a dialogue, and ask them questions, and wait for their answers. Spend time with them and develop a loving, symbiotic relationship with them. This relationship, and the love they provide, will be more fulfilling than any other love relationship you could ever experience. Now, come back into your awareness of your body. Start to take deep breaths, move your feet and hands, and open your eyes. Practice this, and you will begin to step into the wholeness of who you really are, and be fulfilled, needing less, and demanding less from the external world. You will finally have a sense of completeness and wholeness. They will help you in every area of your life. Now that you have met your guides, it is time to start your mediumship work to help others, serve spirit, and serve humanity.

Having a loving relationship with your guides, you will realize you are never alone. I speak to my guides on a regular basis—when I'm driving, at the grocery store, and around the house. They will help you find things that you can't find, lead you to things that are missing, and they will help you in your daily life. You will be amazed. Thank them for their help. Even at the gym, when I am working out hard, and I am trying to do that last push, I have asked them for help. I saw my guide with his hand on my shoulder, and I got through it.

You can also have a "staff meeting." When there is a problem that you are trying to solve, like a health crisis or you are looking for a new job, sit a chair in front of you, and have a staff meeting. They will guide you to whatever is needed. Be open to the way they respond and always give thanks.

Agreements: Feeling Safe as You Begin Your Mediumship Work

Before I go any further, I want to explain agreements. These are agreements with your guides that you set up, and which will help you feel good and safe as you develop your spirit muscle to connect. Some refer to these as boundaries, or "protection." I don't believe in protection, as in the pathway to Heartfelt Mediumship, I believe that protection is rooted in "fear." It feels to me that it stops the natural flow of spirit. Protection means you are feeling fear. Remember, you have a guide that is a protector, so you are already protected. If you need to protect, are you really trusting your angel guides? As we work with spiritual law, you don't want to project any fear as you work with spirit and your guides. Universal law states, "like attracts like," and if we keep our heart open to unconditional love, then we will attract more of the same. Therefore, you can set up agreements with your guides, which are like guard rails, so you feel safe and good as you develop your mediumship. If we truly believe in spiritual law, there are so many times in the ancient scriptures, including the Bible, where we are cautioned against fear. Although you can be fearful in the beginning, and maybe feel some anxiety as you move your energy from the physical world to the spiritual world. It is okay; just acknowledge this, and it will fade over time. Agreements are boundaries that help you develop and feel safe as you are working with your mediumship. You want to stay in the highest vibration while doing this work. And with spirit, there is no fear. I believe that like attracts like. I don't believe that opposites attract. Therefore, to attract love, you must be loving.

Instead of "protection," a better way to think about this is to give yourself a construct that makes you feel comfortable, that doesn't create fear. Setting up agreements with your guides will allow for a natural flow of "feeling good." As you develop your mediumship, agreements allow for unfoldment to occur. These agreements with your guides that are like guard rails to help you stay where you feel comfortable, until you are ready to expand your practice. These agreements are boundaries to help you work with spirit, so you feel safe and feel good, as you want to stay in the most positive energy and the highest vibration. Once you fully develop, you will no longer need boundaries. This will help maintain unconditional love in your heart as you work with spirit. For example, when I first started my mediumship, I had an agreement with my guides that I don't want to be bothered from 10:30 p.m. until 6:00 a.m. Unless there is an emergency, this is my time. They want to come through when our brain is at a relaxed state, when we are sleeping, as this is the time where we are most receptive. But this is your time, and you decide when and how you want to work. You can say things like, "I only work with spirits that are of the highest vibration, that are my guides and my close family members." Because spirits are bound by spiritual law, you have dominion over all of this. A saying in the Christian religion when you want something to depart is "In the name of Jesus, you need to leave." You have the same power and dominion, as this is spiritual law.

On this earth, you can also set boundaries with humans about what is acceptable in your life. One way to set healthy boundaries and adhere to them is to make a list of the things that people may no longer do around you, do to you, or say to you, and what is acceptable—this applies to both spirit people as well as humans. For example, I do NOT like dirty jokes. I don't find them funny, and they are very offensive. There are so many other things to talk about that are humorous.

Another example is not allowing spirit to touch you; this is a boundary. For me, I want to be able to give the clearest evidence for clients, and I allow it, as long as it is about the essence of the spirits' ailments or if it is significant to the evidence of the person coming through for my client. You must determine if this is okay for you. Hopefully, you understand the construct of boundaries and agreements, as they are there to serve you, and your guides help with the adherence to these agreements. Once you are ready to expand yourself to the next level of your mediumship, your guides will know, and you will naturally expand your boundaries to allow additional experiences from spirit.

CHAPTER 3

How Spirit Communicates With Us

To communicate with spirit is a mental exercise—again, not from your logical brain, but the right brain, the imagination, the place where we connect with the "mind." First, I want to clarify that there are two types of mediumship. There is mental mediumship and physical mediumship. For a spirit to physically appear takes more energy to vibrate and hold it, and for us to see it. This happens less frequently than mental mediumship. If you do see a spirit, many times it can be a flash, or they physically appear. The time in which they hold the energy to physically appear can vary. But realize this is more rare than mental mediumship. Most of the time, we will see a person that is in spirit in our mind, and we can see what they are wearing or what they are doing. Spirit speaks to us in pictures. They are flashes and we hold them in our mind; they are not physically in front of us. I will discuss physical mediumship in a later section of this book. These flashes of pictures are coming through quickly because spirit is at a high vibration. We have to train ourselves grab on to the information coming in quickly.

Most mediumship is "mental," and we connect with the super-conscious mind utilizing the right side of the brain, where the infinite intelligence exists. This is where spirit resides. We build the power to make this connection with spirit through meditation. As stated earlier, meditation is the energy to build, hold, and maintain the connection with spirit. It is like the 9-volt battery that you plug in, to give you the energy to connect to the highest vibration. This becomes effortless the more you meditate. And the more you meditate, the stronger your connection to spirit. Meditation makes the connection as you expand your vibration, connect with your soul, and expand your awareness outside of your body.

Psychometry

One of the ways to start to explore your connection is through psychometry. Psychometry is reading the energy of an object and seeing, sensing, and feeling the energy of the person that owned the object. Everyone's energy or aura carries information on historical events, location, and emotions. This energy is transferred to an object. A person can start to read the energy of the object. Everyone can be successful with psychometry. They can hold an object in their hand and start to read the energy. To do an exercise in psychometry, put the object in your left hand, and put your right hand over the object, and close your eyes. You can tap the object and start receiving the information. Make sure your mind is open and allow the information to flow. You will feel various physical aspects of it, and start to get pictures, symbols, and start to sense all the information. Start to deliver all the information you have received about the object, no matter how minuscule you think the information is to the recipient. You can also hold the object to your solar plexus. You will see that by doing this, you will have great success. This exercise will build your confidence in your ability to start to read the information in the energy around objects.

How We Receive Information From Spirit

The way spirit speaks to us has somewhat of a structure as far as the information provided. If you are doing a reading, for example, spirit already knows why they came. The person coming for a reading is called "the sitter" or "the recipient." The structure of my reading is giving information or evidence first, and then I give the message from their loved one. The information comes through is usually circumstances around their death, like an ailment or an accident, the essence of their being, or it could be a specific memory shared with their loved one. This is known as "evidence." Here is a list of types of evidence or information that will come through.

Gender (Male or Female)	Age, Names, Numbers
Relationship to Sitter	Appearance/Description
Personality	Health & Passing Condition
Family & Pets	Occupation & Jobs
Hobbies & Interests	Likes & Dislikes
Habits & Mannerisms	Shared Memories
Objects	Specific Phrases (they always said that!)

No two mediums work alike, nor receive the information the same way. This is what makes your mediumship so unique. Every medium gets information differently, based on their level of frequency and vibration, and if they see, feel, hear, or sense the information. The way a medium receives the information is by hearing, seeing, sensing, feeling, knowing by subtle nudges and cues from the spirit communicator. Your guides and the work you do to learn your "spirit language" takes practice, and your guides will teach you, as well as learn from you, and help you become an effective receiver of information. The key is trusting the information you are getting, and not analyzing it. When you start to analyze the information, your logical mind can get in the way, and then the message from spirit can be misrepresented. Because spirit is at a higher vibration, this information comes through quickly, and meditation will allow your senses to get stronger over time.

As a medium, you have a runner that goes and gets the loved one for your client. Your protector communicates with the runner guide. The runner gets the loved one in spirit. The loved one coming through is called the spirit communicator. The spirit communicator sends the information encoded with symbols you have worked out ahead of time with your guides; you decode the evidence and the message and deliver the message to the recipient.

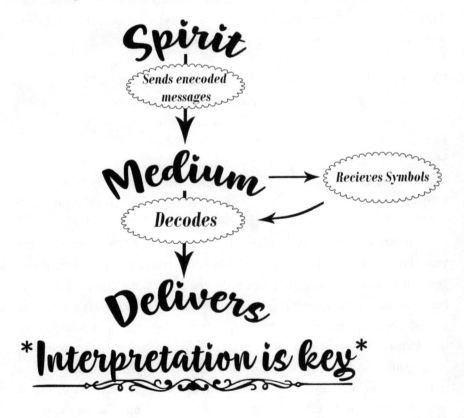

Spirit
Sends enecoded messages

Medium → *Recieves Symbols*
Decodes

Delivers
Interpretation is key

The way mediums receive information is through the "the clairs." Clairs are considered types of mediumship, but I have discovered that spirit will use them all. Many psychics label themselves clairvoyant. You will tend to have roughly two dominant clairs, but all clairs can be used by spirit to present the evidence of their identity. In the beginning, your left brain, or logical thought will intervene and try to make sense out of it. You will question if you are creating this in your imagination. But this is the place where spirit speaks to us. This is where we have developed our connection in meditation to receive this information. This is where you start to utilize your mind and your body as a barometer, as spirit starts to provide information. It comes in the form of these the clairs.

Why is this important? When you are sitting with spirit and they want to convey a message to their loved one, these clairs will start to be utilized. It is up to you, the medium, to start to immediately gather the information, and interpret the message to your client. The key is utilizing all your senses, and be aware of your dominant clair, and start to put the pieces of the puzzle together and deliver the evidence that you are receiving from spirit.

Clairvoyance

The term clairvoyance means "clear seeing" and is the term used when one can see spirit, pictures, or information, in the form of a vision in your head. Obviously, the clarity and detail of the picture you are seeing will vary considerably between individual clairvoyants according to their abilities, some seeing vague somewhat foggy outlines or pictures, and others seeing with startling clarity.

Clairaudience

Clairaudience is "clear hearing" and is the term used when one can hear spirit. It may vary from a vague whisper to a strong and loud voice or other sound such as music or singing, etc. A good clairaudient will easily distinguish pitch, tone, and the emotions of the communicating spirit as well as detecting any accents easily.

Clairaudience is hearing spirit internally or inside the head. Often, this internal "voice," comes in the same form as your own inner voice. Because it comes in the form of your own inner voice, in the early days of development, it is sometimes difficult to discern what is your own inner voice and what is spirit, but the words are usually dropped into you and come quickly. When first learning, it is also much harder to detect accents or emotions of the one communicating, although other gifts such as clairsentience and claircognizance may still enable the medium to sense emotions and accents.

Clairsentience

Clairsentience means "clear feeling," and it is often called empathy. It is the ability to sense or feel spirit physically, emotionally, and energetically. You may feel spirit touch you; this can be anything from a light stroke to firm touch or even a prod or push. You may smell things such as cigar smoke or pipe smoke, or flowers or perfumes, etc.

You may "energetically" feel the touch rather than physically feeling it. Likewise, you may become aware of the emotions of the communicating spirit, feeling their fear, anger, sadness, love, and indeed their happiness and excitement at making contact at last with their loved ones. Sometimes the emotions can be quite overwhelming if the medium is new.

The medium may briefly experience the feelings that the communicating spirit had at the moment of their passing, including the cause of their passing, and they may feel pain in a particular part of the body that represents the pain the person experienced in their last moments, such as chest pain for a heart attack, or head pain in a head trauma or stroke, or the pain of a tumor, or labored breathing for lung condition. None of this should be experienced for more than the moment to enable identification of the person and the cause of their passing. A medium can also experience pain in the right or left hip, where the person had an issue with their hip, even though they didn't pass from this condition. Every range of emotions and physical feelings imaginable can be experienced. Empathy or clairsentience may be challenging for a developing medium that is empathic. When you first start to learn mediumship, you might feel a loss of control over this, but it is important to remember that you are always in control and should determine how much you wish to feel and when. You will learn to allow and control your energy. The loss of control is the resistance instead of allowing. Once you allow and release the energy, you will realize it is not necessary to feel you have to control the process, as you have dominion over all this taking place. Guides will help you. This is part of the agreements you have with your guides and how you want to work. They will adhere to your requests.

Claircognizance

Claircognizance, or "clear knowledge," is when the medium suddenly acquires knowledge of the spirit communicator without seeing, feeling, hearing, or sensing. It is knowledge that appears in the mind of the medium and appears to have no source. It is a pure knowingness without knowing where this sense came from, or how you know this. Mediums who have been practicing for a long time just have a knowing. To quote Tim Brainard, a veteran medium for over fifty years, "You just know. You know that you know that you know. You just know." Those who have this ability will frequently find that they are able to practice the art of inspired writing (not automatic writing—this is something entirely different). Tim writes every day as part of his spiritual practice. I encourage every medium to journal every day, after their meditation. Spirit gives us so much information, and if we don't capture it on paper, we don't fully digest it into our consciousness, and then it is gone.

The knowledge in inspired writing comes fast and is written down by the medium. The reason Tim still journals every day is because spirit speaks to him with wonderful wisdom.

Likewise, many mediums, including Tim, use claircognizance to deliver inspired messages from spirit, whereby instead of writing down the knowledge they speak it in their own voice. Spirit will utilize this with me in my public speaking engagements, as well as sessions with clients.

As with clairvoyance, pictures are dropped into your mind through actual events, symbolic associations, or pieces of information. All spirit communication is based upon the law of love and the vibrational connection with the medium and with the recipient.

Finding Your Dominant Clair

Everyone starting out will have a dominant clair. You can figure out your dominant clair by asking yourself some basic questions. In my class, I provide a 25-question assessment to determine your dominant clair. Spirit usually begins to use all of the clairs, as you start to practice. You can also work on developing the other clairs. Here are some examples of questions to determine your dominant clair. This is just a sample:

1) When you recall a memory of a fantastic vacation, what do you recall?
   A) The way place looked and the views
   B) The sounds of the associated with your vacation
   C) The feelings and sensations associated with your vacation
2) When you are given a task to do, or a job to do, it is easier to carry out if:
   A) I can see what is required or have a visual plan
   B) It is clearly explained to me and I understand it as I sense it
   C) I have a feeling of what's required and a sense of purpose about it
3) When faced with a decision, it helps me to:
   A) Visualize the situation and the choices in my mind's eye
   B) Talk through the situation with friends or colleagues or as a dialogue in my mind
   C) Sense how I feel about the choices and trust my intuition and gut feelings

4) During a discussion with another person, I'm most often influenced by:
   A) Their body language and how I see their point of view
   B) Their tone of voice and how I hear what they are saying
   C) Their body language and how I feel about their point of view

5) Which activities do you prefer? This might be a tough one:
   A) Watching films, visual arts, and reading
   B) Music concerts and good conversation
   C) Physical activities, massage, craft work, and reflection

This is a high-level example, but the full questionnaire ensures your clair dominance. Answers that are mostly A's indicate clairvoyant, mostly B's is clairaudient, mostly C's is clairsentient. But remember, spirit will use any means necessary to provide give evidence to the recipient and deliver messages. I encourage you to can fully develop other the clairs as you study mediumship. You will become proficient in all of them.

The Difference Between being Psychic and a Medium

There are differences between a psychic and a medium. People who are psychic are not necessarily mediums. But all mediums are psychic. The reading is totally different and utilizes different techniques. The psychic connects and holds the link between themselves and the recipient. They usually connect from the solar plexus to the recipient's flow of energy around their body or their aura. The psychic is reading the aura. They may also get information from the recipient's guides and their own guides. But they don't bring forth loved ones in spirit. All answers regarding the person exist in their aura and can be read by a psychic or an intuitive person. Even though information exists in the aura, it is only a glimpse into one's life path, and the recipient can choose to go on a different path, so it really doesn't account for free will. However, a psychic can see job offers, people coming into their lives, people leaving, struggles, and life path information, to guide the recipient.

A medium connects with spirit and brings forth loved ones by connecting upward and all around us while holding the psychic link. Sometimes the medium can drop the psychic link, depending on the attitude of the recipient, and you just connect with spirit, if you have a cynic or a skeptic. A great medium doesn't need the psychic connection to give evidence and messages. A medium who is starting out or just learning mediumship might need both links.

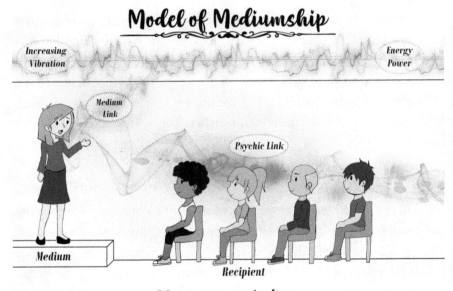

Model of Mediumship

Increasing Vibration

Energy Power

Medium Link

Psychic Link

Medium

Recipient

Messages to an Audience

Mediumship is a complex process and depends on many factors. It is always experimental and there are no guarantees of the outcome. Successful mediumship depends on the communicator (the spirit coming through), the medium, the audience/recipient, the venue, and the format. All these factors are interrelated and cannot be viewed in isolation. It can depend on the medium's emotional and mental state, training, attitude and ego, power to connect, preparation and planning, personality, professionalism, trust in spirit, and confidence in his/her ability. Similar factors come into play for the communicator in spirit and the recipient and audience. Never work when you are tired or exhausted. When working, always have a great mental attitude, and I always tell my recipient/audience to send me love. Love is the highest vibration and it helps to connect with spirit.

CHAPTER 4

Structure of a Reading

When we sit down to do a reading, many factors enter into it. The medium must be prepared and in a good place where they are in tune with the infinite consciousness (the God Source). This is the highest vibration of love. You know when you are attuned because you will feel light, and everything is effortless. You can smile easily because you feel the love connection with the infinite. Invite your guides into the reading and invite the recipient's guides in to facilitate the reading. Then, drop into your heart and feel the love of your heart expressing outward toward the recipient. I always say a quick prayer, as it helps me to connect with my recipient's guides. I recommend you always say a prayer that you memorize, as it is a ritual that you use to connect with spirit. I ask for them to say their name, to hear the vibration, and then I say the prayer. My prayer is: "Father, Mother God, I come before you and give thanks and praise for all the blessings received, both seen and unseen. We are so grateful. I ask that my guides connect with (recipient's name's) guides, and we bring forth evidence of loved ones, and messages of guidance, upliftment, healing, and reassurance. And with this, I say, AMEN." If you want, and I find this is personal preference, you connect with the recipient's energy, after connecting with the divine, so you are holding both links. Once these links are established, which takes only a few moments, the reading begins.

While this is occurring, every medium has a runner that goes and gets the loved ones. The loved ones will give the evidence and bring forth messages of guidance, healing, upliftment, and reassurance. There is never any negative information given. They come through with lots of unconditional love, forgiveness, understanding, apologies, and healing. The "runner" could have already arranged this, even days before the reading, and could have already been set up prior to the recipient arriving. I've had spirit communicators arrive before the recipient.

The medium brings forth the evidence previously discussed, as this establishes who is coming through with the message. The evidence is very personal and will establish the essence of the person in spirit. When first starting out, I always wrote things down that I was getting. The reason for this is because if I saw it, or sensed it, I wrote it down, then it happened. Then I gave what I got. It was a way of building trust in what I was seeing. If I wrote it down, it happened. Then my left brain could not jump in and analyze it. I would say, "Did I just see that?" "Did I really see that?" Uncertainty, fear, and doubt would creep in and the connection would be lost. We need to stay in connection with our right brain that connects to the infinite consciousness. It seems like it is imagination, but it is not. If a picture is dropped into your mind, then it is spirit. It is up to you, the medium, to translate the information.

Once you have delivered the evidence, then spirit always brings forth a message of guidance, healing, upliftment, and reassurance. If it is not information that falls into these categories, then I doubt it is a message from spirit; it is more of the opinion of the medium. Please feel and know what is being communicated and deliver it. The delivery of the message is of a pure heart. This is why it is very important to commit to self-development. You do not want to taint the message from spirit with your own baggage or your own stories. You must work hard to get rid of judgement, control, anger, and resentment, because when spirit comes through, it is with unconditional love. You want to be able to trust and able to share the information from the purest of heart. I will speak more about this later, regarding delivery of messages to your recipient. But the point here is to deliver with the purest intentions and represent spirit in the way the message is intended.

Evidence may come in the form of symbols, literal information, association, sensing, and feeling. Spirit speaks to us many forms. They use energy and vibration to create the information, symbols etc., to deliver to the medium, and the medium must discern, decipher, decode, and deliver the information to the recipient. This information is shared through the mind of the medium, while the medium is connected with spirit. You can ask questions in your mind to get the information, and you can ask them to slow down while spirit is giving the information. If you don't see it, or it came through quickly, you can ask for them to slow down and give it again.

This is where practice comes in. Mediums must give the information coming in literally. If the recipient doesn't recognize it, then it can be a symbol, or it can be something they figure out later after the reading. But it is not about giving the symbol to the recipient. It is about you, the medium, interpreting the symbol and giving the message behind the symbol. For example, one time a medium said to me, "I see three rings around you. Two have been given to you, and one hasn't been given yet." If I weren't a medium, I would have been left in bewilderment. I was left to interpret, and I knew what that meant because spirit explained it to me in the moment she gave it to me. I was in the audience, so I couldn't ask questions. Please do not leave your recipient or audience wondering about a symbol. That symbol is for the medium to interpret and give the message. You have to follow it all the way through, by interpreting the symbol and delivering the message from spirit.

Symbols

Symbols are images that spirit will utilize to describe something for the recipient. You work these out ahead of time, meditating and praying on these images and working with your guides. This takes practice. I have a notebook of symbols where I wrote down images that either spirit gave me, or I gave spirit to tell them how to describe either circumstances or the essence or personalities of people coming through. Know that these can be intertwined with literal information.

For example, I might see a man or feel/sense a man, and he has on suspenders. Suspenders is my symbol for a grandfather. I would ask, "On mother's or father's side?" I would see my mother. Then I would see an elephant. An elephant is my symbol for thick-skinned, memory like an elephant, and a high level of understanding. Maybe he also showed me what he did for a living; he showed me a farm. Suddenly, I would get an overwhelming sense of love. Then I heard a nickname, "Kiki." So I would give this as: "I have a grandfather in spirit; he says he is from your mother's side of the family. He is showing me he was thick-skinned, with a keen memory, and he is showing me a farm. I sensed he worked on this farm, and he was very fond of you and loved you so much. He just gave me a nickname, Kiki—do you understand this?"

You can get yes on some of it and no on some. Say you get a no on the farm—is this a symbol? Or is this something the recipient doesn't know? You can ask spirit. Try to get the answer before you move on. Then ask spirit for the message. What is the message? They start to give more information. it could be things happening in the recipient's life and they are around guiding them, or the recipient is worried about a decision, and spirit gives them guidance. Structure the message and deliver it in the way spirit intended the message. Be loving, articulate, and have a level of accountability and responsibility with what you deliver, with the highest level of ethics. We will go more into the delivery of the evidence and message, but this is a quick tip and guidance here. The difference between a good medium and a great medium is not only the strong connection with spirit that builds over time, but it also the verbiage used to describe what you are seeing, sensing, feeling, hearing. Please try never use the verbiage, "I am picking up," or "pick up." You are "sensing, hearing, seeing, feeling." Also, never use the words "think," or I think that…." This refers to your left brain, where it is coming in to analyze the information you are getting. This is not an analysis.

As you work with spirit, and practice, the activity will create the knowledge, but for now, let's discuss symbols. Symbols are free-flowing and something that is meaningful to you. When you first start out, you give it literally, and if means nothing to the recipient, then you give it symbolically. You will then start to discern what are your symbols and what is literal evidence. The list of symbols is endless. What I recommend to my students is to carve out time where you work on your symbols with spirit. Keep a journal handy and write out things maybe that you have seen or want to make your symbol. You can start by segmenting three columns. The first column is the symbol itself, the second column is what it means to you, and the third column is what you are sensing, feeling, seeing, or hearing. This will come through usually with your dominant clair. This is also an exercise where you can expand your clairs. As you work with the symbols, for example, if your dominant clair is clairvoyance, then you will be able to see it clearly. But you might also want to ask the question "What else am I sensing or feeling?" You should have symbols for relationships, symbols describing personality, life situations, and timing. Many mediums use animals to represent traits of a person. Here are a few examples, but you must come up with your own. These are very personal, and you create your own symbols with spirit:

Symbol	Meaning	Seeing, feeling, hearing, sensing
Female	Communicator	Sensing vibration energy on left side
Male	Communicator	Sensing vibration energy on right side
Apron	Grandmother	Seeing a pink apron with flowers
Suspenders	Grandfather	Seeing a man with suspenders
My Dad with Hat	Father	Seeing my dad in a Hawaiian hat
My Mom	Mother	Seeing a pic of my mother at a fountain
Margaret	Mother-in-law	Seeing my aunt's mother-in-law
Uncle Bob	Uncle Bob Gehman	Seeing my uncle Bob, sensing healing
Girl in Dress	Daughter	Seeing girl in a dress, sensing purity
Doublemint Gum	Twin	Seeing a stick of gum, feeling double
Ring with Slash	Divorce	Seeing ring with a slash through it
Red Heart	Girlfriend or boyfriend	Seeing a red heart, sensing love
Rabbit	Authentic, innocent	Bunny, soft, light energy
Abe Lincoln	Honest, trustworthy	See Abe, sense tall, or breakdown
Lion	Courageous	Seeing lion, sensing dignity
Eagle	High performer	soaring with eagles, sets sights high
Elephant	Thick-skinned	See elephant, sense characteristics
Dog	Literal, or companionship	Seeing dog, or feeling companionship
Cup	Happiness	Seeing cup, sensing being happy
Syringe	Overdose	Seeing a syringe, sensing & discerning
Blood drop	Diabetes	Seeing drop of blood, sensing tingling
Pink Ribbon	Breast Cancer	Seeing ribbon, pain in chest
Wedding dress	Wedding	Seeing wedding dress
Scrubs	Nurse	Seeing scrubs, sensing occupation
White Coat	Doctor	Seeing lab coat, sensing intelligence
Teddy Bear	Healing	Sensing healing with recipient

Spirit utilizes these symbols that you work out in advance. Remember, these are YOUR symbols, and no one else's. You work with your spirit guides in advance. Meditate or also see what comes to mind, or it could be that you feel a certain way. Whatever way you receive this information, you should know this in advance—you should be able to describe what you are feeling. Just as you trust spirit, spirit trusts you to deliver the evidence to the recipient. The symbols are examples of my symbols. You can use these symbols or create your own. But you will need to practice delivering the evidence. Take these relationships, life situations, characteristics of the spirit communicator, and string together the evidence. As the medium, it's like putting the pieces of a puzzle together to draw a picture. The evidence helps describe the uniqueness of this person, discern whether it is literal or symbolic, and describe the essence of the spirit communicator.

If you have done tarot cards in the past with your psychic work, and you have a deck that you like, spirit can use these pictures from the deck in your mind, as well, to describe certain life situations. For example, if the ace of cups means to you that happiness is forthcoming and it is overflowing, spirit can drop this picture of the ace of cups in your mind, and you can deliver this message. But I really encourage you, for the purposes of mediumship, to trust spirit, not utilize your cards. This is dropping from a mediumship link into a psychic link. Remember, you are working on your mediumship. I am using this only as a potential example of spirit utilizing any picture in your mind to bring forth a message.

I have a journal of symbols that I visit in my meditation, so they become clear. Activity will create the knowledge for you. For example, with my symbols, if I sense a male spirit, and I see suspenders, and then I see a teddy bear, I would say to the recipient, "I have your grandfather here and he is showing me a teddy bear. Does this mean anything to you?" Maybe the recipient received a teddy bear. If they say no, you still must hold the link with spirit and revisit the meaning of a teddy bear. This meaning of a teddy bear is specifically for you as a medium, so if you have worked this out ahead of time and teddy bear is on your list, you can then deliver it. So maybe I am sensing they are concerned about a health issue, or they are afraid because they will be going into surgery. The spirit communicator shows me a teddy bear. I know that they will be healing just fine and everything will be okay. So, I deliver the message that everything will go well with their upcoming surgery. I also have an Indian chief that comes through when someone is going to have surgery. He always appears when shows everything will go better than expected, and usually the doctors are seeing things that are close to miraculous. This Indian chief is amazing, as he comes through every time when something wonderfully miraculous is going to happen.

Another way to add to your evidence is by reading books on different subjects like gardening or a book of names. Spirit can show you a particular flower, for example. Instead delivering the message of "spirit is showing me flowers," wouldn't it be more powerful if "a grandmother is coming through and she is showing me blue hydrangeas"?

Similarly, by studying a book of names, you can get names more effectively from spirit. You can certainly ask spirit for the name, but if you are more clairvoyant, you might see the name on the page that you read or studied.

As a medium, the more time you spend in studying various topics of life, nature, travel and other experiences, you will add value, giving the best reading for your clients.

Delivering the Message

After delivering the evidence, and describing the essence of the communicator, there is always a message that is associated with the spirit communicator. Always, the message is uplifting, reassuring, guiding, comfort, and healing. Only one time did I receive a warning, and it was for a family member, and I sensed it so strongly. Prophetically, it came true, but I really did my best to warn the family member. I have never received another warning so strongly than I did with the person closest to me. Most always, spirit is coming from the highest vibration of unconditional love and peace. They will come through with apologies, asking for forgiveness, forgiveness for the recipient, guidance, comfort, love, helping them release guilt, anger, grief, to set the recipient free of any negativity and give them the comfort to continue on their life journey. It can be so freeing, life-changing, healing, and nothing short of powerful and miraculous. Never should there be any prophetic message of doom and gloom. And there are ethical considerations, as well. We NEVER predict someone's passing. Even if you feel it, it is NOT up to you. This is between God and that person to determine when they "go home." If someone is delivering information that is NOT guidance and uplifting, then I say that this is the medium's opinion, or where he/she is at in their self-development, and this message is NOT coming from the highest vibration. Anything that will cause fear, doubt, and uncertainty is NOT coming from spirit. A warning could come, but it is in the form of love and helping them navigate and guide. Never does it come from fear, uncertainty, and doubt. The message is always empowering and uplifting and can provoke deep thought on the part of the recipient. Therefore, we must deliver the message with the highest ethics, morals, and values, with a level of accountability and responsibility, that we are representing spirit, and it is NOT our opinion. Therefore self-development is so important. There are mediums that are prophetic, but I would keep a journal of prophetic insights and see if they come true. This takes years of prayer and meditation. Spirit entrusts this information to you. All the while, collectively, we have free-will that can change the course of actions.

The Essence of Your Spirit

Being a great medium is also about the essence of your spirit. I want you to think about what makes you unique. You are the culmination of all your life experiences that make up who you are, and your self-development has added to the essence of your being. When delivering messages, you want to deliver from the highest, most authentic, and purest form of yourself. This is what makes my mediumship—and everyone's mediumship—so unique. It is why people are drawn to you. They feel connected and they feel the sweetness of your spirit. When you are delivering your messages and blending with spirit, you are now spirit, so feel it, embrace it, and allow this to be shown to your clients. If you are judging yourself, not feeling worthy, or have ego involved in any way, the essence of your being will not come forth. You really must be connected and allow it to flow from your being naturally. People will feel this and connect with it naturally. There are skeptics, but you do not have to allow their attitudes to change who you are or your connection with spirit. If you keep your connection with spirit and do worry about someone else's perception of you (again, this is ego and left brain, so don't go there), trust spirit to create the sweetness in the room. They will experience something unique and beautiful that only spirit can create through you.

We have spent a lot of time on process, but I assure you that after allowing spirit in, and blending with spirit, the essence of your being will flow so beautifully. It takes practice, and spending time in meditation to develop, but your unique essence will make this experience unique and beautiful for the recipient.

Self-Development

Understanding psychology is so important. Having a wealth of knowledge is also knowing of where to guide people to get additional help. This might include other practitioners, healers, and other places that you know are certified to help these individuals. You must be committed to your own self-development, as a medium, as a person, and making sure your life is in order, and not a "train wreck." How can you possibly guide clients if you haven't taken care of your own life? For example, when I was younger, I practiced martial arts, and I learned that the instructor should be a role model for his/her students. Instructors themselves train so they can physically do more than they demand of their students. They would never expect their students to do 50 push-ups when they personally could only do ten! It is expected that they are able to do three times more than their students. They must model the behavior that they expect of their students. Model the behavior of self-discipline, dignity, and accountability. If you have money issues in your life, for example, spend time learning about money, the flow of money, your relationship with money, the universal and spiritual principles about money, and expand your consciousness about money before you give financial advice. See areas of your life which you need to overcome and start working on those areas, so you can be a role model. Your goal is to be a role model for spirit and represent spirit well.

Practice Being Articulate

It is important that you practice expressing what you are sensing. There are many ways to do this during your day. This can be done in the car. Remember playing "I SPY" in the car on a road trip when you were a kid? You can do this in your mind, as well. "I see…" and articulate it, then express what you are sensing. Also, you are able to do this while meditating. It is always recommended to keep a journal and express what you are seeing, sensing, and feeling after meditation. Spirit gives us all kinds of information while we are driving, doing mundane tasks, or while we are in meditation. Make sure you write it down, so you can grab on to the thoughts and pictures they are showing you. If you don't write it down, you will not remember, as spirit inspiration tends to leave us after it is given. I've heard this referred to as psychic amnesia.

Spirit Inspiration

According to Webster's dictionary, https://www.merriam-webster.com/words-at-play/the-origins-of-inspire, the word Inspire "has an unusual history in that its figurative sense appears to predate its literal one. It comes from the Latin inspiratus (the past participle of inspirare, 'to breathe into, inspire') and in English has had the meaning "the drawing of air into the lungs" since the middle of the 16th century." I believe the true origin of the word inspiration comes from "in spirit." Spirit can bring forth inspiration to us, when our mind is open and ready to receive. It doesn't have to be just in meditation. While doing mundane tasks, in the shower, or driving down the road, keep your mind open. For example, I was in meditation and I have been studying leaky gut and leaky brain syndrome. Then I was in my car, parking my car at the grocery store, and I heard from spirit, "leaky wallet syndrome." I have been studying the flow of money, money consciousness and understanding spiritual laws of money. I took this as a sign that spirit wants me to do a class or write a book on the spiritual principles of money. Spirit gives us inspiration. So, make sure you write it down, to not only practice being articulate in your message-giving, but also to record every inspiration from spirit.

CHAPTER 5

Morals and Ethics

$\mathcal{A}$ny person who deals or works with people in any way while providing a service is responsible to know the laws of the country that you reside in, which regulates the protection of you and your clients.

These are some basic ethics, morals, and values that you should educate yourself about and get familiar with, and use your common sense to make sure you have the highest ethics and are being responsible to you and your clients. I am spending time on this to provide you with knowledge to be responsible toward yourself and toward your clients/sitters/recipients. Always have a disclaimer that states that this is for entertainment purposes only. It should also say that you are not a doctor, and any decisions that your client makes is based upon sound mind, and they take full responsibility for their decisions. I recommend looking at disclaimers in books on nutrition, and other disclaimers, and make sure your disclaimer is reviewed. I have my disclaimer posted on my website, and wherever I do readings. I am a spiritualist and practice under the expectations of this being spiritual counseling. But many do not do this and can be irresponsible with clients. I've heard of psychics telling people that their loved ones are stuck in tunnels because they can't connect with them, or the recipient has a curse and they will charge them $2500 to remove the curse. This is absurd. Please be aware of local, state, and national laws.

Here are some do's and don'ts. The main thing is NEVER provide information that may be harmful to your client or yourself in any way. You must be VERY responsible in delivering the message. Your guides are there to guide you and might tell you not to read for someone. You must listen to this and follow your heart.

All readings MUST be kept confidential. Do not share a reading with your mother, your sister, a friend of your sitter, or their spouse. It is unethical to do so. A client comes to you for a private reading, and this is what you ensure when you accept this person as a client. This requires complete anonymity. There are exceptions to this, if the client has told you that they plan to harm themselves or someone else. It is YOUR responsibility to give this person their local crisis hotline number and end the reading. Make a list of all area crisis numbers and have them handy. You must know your limitations as a medium and know that they need professional help, which is beyond your service offering. Also, if you are being mentored, and you have questions about evidence, or a particular situation with a client, as long as it is kept confidential and you are utilizing this to become more effective in mediumship, then it is ok to share this with your mentor.

Ensure that the information given to the recipient is positive and uplifting. It should be solution oriented. Spirit speaks in guidance, upliftment, and reassurance. This needs to be reflected in the delivery of your reading. You want your client to have a wonderful experience from the reading and leave feeling lighter, happier, and with a greater sense of peace than when they first came to you for a reading.

Commit to self-development. Educate yourself, and continually work through life issues; this is crucial to our work with spirit. Sometimes spirit brings people to you who are working on the exact life issues which you have mastered. Know that you are spirit too, and spirit brought them to you because you have practical ways to help them through the negative thoughts, emotions, or life experiences. This is where you are spirit, and you guide them and give them practical solutions and a path forward. Spirit is trusting you to do this. Spirit can also bring clients that are going through a similar life circumstance, and they give you the solution, along with the client. After doing many readings, I have found that because of my business experience, and being a single parent for many years, spirit brings me these two types of clients regularly. Just remember where you were when you were going through a similar crisis. Embrace it, and feel it, because this is exactly where your client is and you must meet them where they are, not where you are since you overcame the issue. You might have the key to the step-by-step process to lift them out of their life circumstance. Reading for them is great, but you also want to give them tools so when they leave you, they can continue to grow and stay uplifted and positive. Have a list of books or resources that might help guide and navigate them through this life issue. Continue your development, reading, and ongoing study. You want to constantly keep learning how to best help your clients with books, articles, and information that they can read and research long after their session.

Never predict death or an accident. If during a reading you become aware of something that may feel like death, it serves no useful purpose to terrify or upset your client with this news. We do not always hear spirit correctly, as we are human and doing our best to align with the energies. Besides, this is between them and God. Never, never predict death or someone's passing. Even if you feel it with your heart and soul, never predict it, as the timing of a person's transition is out of your hands. Besides, spirit views this as something wonderful—they are going home. It is through our human eyes that we judge death as something horrible. Spirit shared with me that we judge things from a human perspective but coming home is a wonderful, peaceful, and loving experience. Spirit shared with me that Trajectory of life is an expectation. Expectations fool the heart and cause the loss of one's soul. Reflect and re-visit your expectations, for these are not spiritual. They are human. We must lift ourselves up to a new level of understanding.

As for accidents, is it associated with a spirit who has crossed over, or with something forthcoming? If you know that there might be an accident forthcoming, but it could be that the person has anxiety about accidents, deliver the information in a way that it can be helpful. I don't ever feel comfortable predicting actual accidents, as it only serves to cause heightened fear. Spirit is not about fear. I personally have never received messages like this except one time with a family member. This is NOT my focus as a medium, and I really would stay clear of this. The power of suggestion and universal principle can start a heightened sense of fear which can bring forth the accident, instead of avoiding it. Would you like to receive this information from a medium? I wouldn't, and how long do you wait for an accident? Again, this could be as-sociated with the circumstances of the spirit passing. Please steer clear of giving information like this and check your interpretation of the evidence. Think first of how you would take information given to you in this way. Many times, I will say to a client, "Are you having issues with your [fill in the blank]," or, "Have you had this checked recently? Spirit is telling me that all will be well, but might check into this, as this might require your attention, okay?"

In addition, NEVER Dress as a madam or some other mystical person. I always dress professionally and want to be warm and ap-proachable. I want people to feel comfortable and loved when they are in my presence. I see people dressing up to play the part of the old-time gypsies. While it's fun for Halloween parties and sometimes especially for theme parties, in normal everyday work, it only makes us look weird or fake. You want to represent yourself well; do this by dressing nicely and showing self-care, as this reflects that you care for others as well. Dress professionally and not wacky. You are representing spirit, not your "egotistical free spirit self." Your appearance is just as important as the messages you deliver. Also, when you go professional, your name is your integrity—what do your name and brand say about you? Calling yourself 44 Feathers Mystic Dragon Goddess does not build your reputation as a reader, and it also sends up red flags to the community. Be yourself and be authentic and confident. Respect is necessary, so show yourself some self-respect and dignity. Universal law says you will attract more of the same. You will then attract people who respect you and treat you with dignity.

Please don't prescribe or diagnose. We are not medical doctors and must never pretend to be, but if you want to share your own experience, it is okay to do so. I have experience with certain supplements. I share with clients my experience with supplements that have been helpful for me, but I ask them to do their own research and check with their medical doctor. I share it only from the perspective of my personal experience. Just let them know that you are not a medical doctor and to do their own research. People sometimes ask me about their health or medical condition. If they ask me a medical question, I always suggest that they see their general practitioner. I might give a referral to a practitioner, based upon my own experience. But I always ask them to do their own research and see if it resonates with them as a possible solution. I may sense things, but I make sure they know I'm not a medical professional. Spirit has shown me many times that everything will be alright in an upcoming surgery. I do pass along this message, as it is comforting and healing.

Don't ever predict the future. As mediums/psychics, we can see only potential futures, and some of the information may not be available in full detail to us. Also, this might be only one path, as everyone has free will. You can say things like "I feel your father in spirit is trying to tell you that he is supportive of you going back to school. See if that resonates with you." That way, you are empowering the recipient to make their own decisions, rather than saying, "You will go back to school and study psychology." Be careful because these "prediction" readings will come back haunt you when you are wrong.

At the back of the book, I have shared the code of conduct law from the UK and some other information from the US UC Code on Fraudulent Statements. Take time to read through this, but bringing forth messages of spirit, you will deliver messages with integrity, honesty, and the highest level of accountability.

CHAPTER 6

Challenges with your Mediumship, Messages, Recipients, and Audiences

There are many factors affecting your mediumship. These factors can be related to you the medium, the spirit communicator, the recipient or the audience, the venue, or the format. These factors can be interrelated, and you cannot view them in isolation. For the purposes of this discussion, it is more about identifying the issues what you can do about them. If you plan to do this work long term, you will encounter issues, so you need to recognize them. The difference between a good medium and a great medium is how they manage and solve problems with their mediumship.

There are different problems that are faced by beginning, intermediate, and advanced mediums. Whatever you encounter, do not make stuff up to get out of the situation. Be honest and authentic, but most importantly, meditation helps build the ability to connect. If you build your ability to connect, you will always be able manage any issues.

Spirit will help you.

The issues for the medium could be their training, knowledge, ability to connect with spirit, their motivation, presentation and appearance, their preparation, and their trust and confidence in their ability. In addition, it can be how they are feeling, their mental and emotional state, whether they have been overworked, and the use of alcohol. As a medium, you have the most control over managing yourself, versus the variables of the audience, recipient, the communicator, and the venue and format.

The other challenge can be the spirit communicator, but your guides can help manage this. Sometimes they can have a very subtle personality, when there are other spirits that come in loud and clear. Some mediums interpret that the person is not there when he/she is just doesn't have the ability to communicate effectively. This could be the essence of their spirit while on earth. In addition, spirit also must learn how to communicate through a medium. They also must understand the reason for their communication.

With the venue, it might be too cold, or too hot, or there could be loud noises when you are presenting. The atmosphere and physical area might be not ideal. But as a medium, you have control over your ability.

To manage these factors, always establish a rapport with the recipient or an audience. With an audience, you can tell a joke to get everyone laughing. This raises the vibration in the room. I always ask the audience to send me love, as I know this will help with my connection. As I start to speak, the environment melts away, and I focus on spirit and the recipient. Always be respectful and professional. In platform mediumship, if it is too difficult to work, or if you have found that you have lost your link with spirit, take time to teach a little and give snippets on how spirit speaks to us, until your link is re-established. I have been with audiences where it was expected for me to hold my link for two hours and give readings. When I sensed my link would drop, I would have information, stories of spirit and ways to teach, as I re-established my link. This was a lesson learned, not to allow anyone to book me for two hours. If you accept this type of booking, be very prepared, knowing how long you can hold your link, and bring other material to help establish credibility of your work.

Working with Recipients

When people come for a reading, I get their permission to read for them and I confirm this with them, even though they scheduled the reading. I ask them to say their name, as this helps me to connect with spirit, through hearing the vibration of their voice. Please be sensitive and loving to the recipient, and take into consideration their emotional and mental state, any language barriers, any physical disabilities. And always give the recipient time to respond. I have seen mediums become demanding, upset with their recipient, demanding a response right away. I have witnessed this, and this can be downright rude. There is no reason to pressure the recipient, when they are trying to process what you are saying. Never bully or embarrass the recipient, ever! I have seen this done by mediums on stage. I have also seen them demand a response and get frustrated if someone doesn't answer right away. I don't understand this, as spirit is kind and gentle. You should be kind and gentle too. Be confident in the information that spirit is giving you and be gracious and courteous. If they are not getting it, and you have worked with the communicator to get all the evidence for now, you can just say, "We will park that for now." It is very common that this can hit them later—a day or two, or even a week. Just trust the information from spirit. Always work with a positive attitude, and always be prepared. Avoid working when you are physically ill, under the influence of alcohol, or under significant emotional or mental stress.

When you receive unclear replies from the recipient, we tend to question what is going on, and our left brain comes in to analyze it. We also then start to lose our link. When we get a "no," for example, we start to create doubt in our own mind, and we can lose confidence. We can fall into a place where we fall to pieces and lose our link. Always stay connected and don't worry about the response. Stay with the evidence and work to identify it, and if it is not working, then we park it and move on, all the while holding our link to spirit. But don't give up on a "no" response. Let's discuss working with the "no's."

Working With No's

Get used to hearing no's because they are going to happen. You will develop a level of confidence where the no's won't bother you. They are part of the feedback and information. You can give a piece of evidence and you give it literally and symbolically, and you still get a no. Sometimes people don't realize it until maybe a week later but didn't understand it at the time. Be willing to work with the no's; redirect and clarify. Sometimes a "no" just means you need to deliver the evidence or symbol differently, which can be more powerful, and resonate more with your recipient. Or, they might have an "aha" moment after they leave, up to a week later. This "no" could be a set up for a redelivery of the information that could be extremely profound. Remember to always trust spirit and what they give you to deliver. The key is interpret the information correctly. Always trust spirit. Spirit is never wrong.

Tips for the Recipient

A medium cannot always the access the person in spirit that the recipient wants to connect with initially. The recipient needs to be in a good state of mind, relaxed and open-minded. You might want to connect with someone in spirit, and you might be looking for a specific piece of evidence that you want from your loved one. Just remain open. Set your intention with spirit prior to the reading, and make your specific requests known to them. Be open and give feedback, as this also helps the flow of information from the spirit communicator and strengthens the connection. Be open to receive the information. Send love to the medium to help strengthen the link.

Platform Mediumship

Platform mediumship is another way in which readings are given. These are readings given to an audience. These are also referred to as gallery reads. Platform mediumship is part of the service in the Spiritualist Church and is part of the service to demonstrate the continuity of life. There are mediums within the church or visiting mediums that give platform demonstrations. Many mediums provide platform demonstrations as part of their service work for the church and serving spirit. When mediums are of service, spirit works with the medium on platform to teach them, and become more open to spirit. As you are utilized as an instrument, spirit will continue to find ways of service for you. Make sure you set your intention for spirit to come through clearly. When you set your intention with spirit, it is important that you have experience in giving messages from the platform. Platform readings are brief, with evidence and messages of guidance, healing, and reassurance. Make sure that you have the appropriate social filter, only giving evidence that is appropriate in a public demonstration. We must show compassion and be gentle with our audience. There are issues with doing platform reads. It could run smoothly, but there are challenges that you may have to navigate.

Here are a few things to be aware of, but know that you can work through them. You might get bombarded with evidence, or more than one spirit communicator at one time. Stick with it to sort it out. Tell spirit, "Only one at a time, please." Or you get more than one person thinking it is their loved one. The key is to get more evidence from spirit to sort out which person the spirit communicator belongs to in the audience.

You might stand up there and you can have no spirit communicator, or a living communicator, which happens sometimes with loved ones who have Alzheimer's. Alzheimer's patients can come through as if they are in spirit. You can also have a link and no one in the audience claims the person, and there is silence. If this happens, I tell my guide that I am moving on. I will always say, "We will park this for now." I have found that if this happens, the recipient doesn't want to claim the loved one due to being shy, or not wanting to receive a message from spirit in a public forum.

The key is to trust the evidence you receive from spirit. Also, stay with your strongest evidence and work it. Give the evidence as you receive it. Always stay with spirit, and don't worry about the audience. Don't allow yourself to go to a psychic link; stay with the medium link with spirit. Monitor your link and always check your evidence with the recipient. Don't give too much evidence and use a social filter in public. You might have to filter what you say to the recipient, but always give a beautiful, uplifting message.

If you are on platform, don't give up; most mediums give up too soon, and you must work hard to place the communicator with the right person. But also, don't force it to fit. Again, give enough evidence for a recipient to identify the communicator, and outline of the message. If there are no takers of the message, then move on. We also must accept that sometimes we have to things go, if we can't find the recipient, or if the recipient stays silent. This happens to everyone. Always be honest and never make things up or blame anyone.

CHAPTER 7

— ❧ —

Closing the Door to Spirit

When you are ready to work with spirit and your guides, unlock this door and invite your guides and spirit. I say a quick prayer that signals my guides that it is time to work. I also take my clients into prayer, so they are open and receptive. This signals spirit that it is time to work, and I imagine them all coming into the room with me.

After your day of spirit communication, you then will need to close the door and disconnect from the link. However, always remain open to spirit. Make sure you thank all your guides and spirits and watch them leave to the other side. I always say a closing prayer to let them know I am done with the communication. But they always know and the energy drops. It is a mutual thing; they and I both know when it is done. My main guide may remain with me if she chooses. I believe my main guide helps me back to the state of being on this earth.

Grounding and Clearing

We all belong to the earth, and we must create balance again, by connecting to the earth's frequency. If we've had a full day of readings, we will need to clear the energy by breathing. Taking deep breaths to fill the body with oxygen is so important, along with drinking water. Water and oxygen are elements of the earth that helps re-establish our connection with the earth, where we belong. We connect with the earth and our bodies through these elements.

After doing a day's work, I always ground and clear. Grounding helps to disconnect from the spirit world, and grounds me to the earth. Remember that the earth resonates at 8.37 Hz. We must bring our vibration back down to the earth's frequency. Because spirits are at the highest vibration, we must release and clear all of the energy that has been absorbed during the reading.

Every day we absorb energy and we send energy, whether it's on the telephone, on social media, or wherever we go. Doing this can drain you or cause you to have too much energy in your system. When you have too much energy you may feel ill or restless, or maybe you can't sleep. After a day of many reads, I have gotten sick the next morning. Depletion of energy is the opposite; you may feel depressed, sick, sad, out of sorts and extremely tired.

By learning to ground your energy and release it into the earth, and pull up energy from our earth, you can help to balance your life and feel much better right away. Calling back your energy is important, and you can do this quickly. After three to five minutes, you will feel much better. The way you clear your energy, is to go outside, stand in the grass barefoot, and breathe. During the winter, I still go outside and stand on the ground; I lift my hands up the air in an arching motion, and take a big breath in, and drop my arms on the exhale. I repeat this four to five times. I imagine mother earth opening a portal by my feet, and I send all the energy that doesn't belong to me into the earth for healing. I breathe deep breaths and send the energy through my body. This is simple way to ground and clear your energy. I've also invested in a grounding pad, which is roughly $250, which I have on my bed to help me ground. It has made a great difference in me being able to ground. Also, make sure you drink plenty of water.

CHAPTER 8

―❦―

Physical Mediumship vs. Mental Mediumship

*M*ost of the information I have provided in this book is regarding mental mediumship. The most famous and well known are recognized because of many TV series that have been developed to showcase the physical phenomena, and people become frightened. The producers of these shows put a "scary" music score, and voilà! You have people freaking out and tuning in for more. Most people concentrate on the phenomena versus the philosophy. The philosophy, science, and religion behind all forms of mediumship is that there is something beyond this world that we strive to understand. Spirit communication between this world and the unseen world demonstrates the continuity of life, that there is no death, and the medium brings forth this evidence by all forms of mediumship for guidance, healing, upliftment, and reassurance.

Remember that we work with the natural laws of frequency, vibration, and energy. Spirit does, too. Physical mediumship is when a spirit manipulates energy. To do this, a spirit uses the energy from the psychic medium to create phenomena that can be seen, heard, or felt by everyone present. The spirit uses the medium as a "power source." It can happen with people who aren't mediums. For example, when we are stressed, suddenly there are raps and taps. This a loved one potentially who wants to say hello and get you to re-focus your energy on something positive, or to let you know that they are there watching over you. Another example of a loved one saying hello is when lights flicker on and off. It's common for spirits to be there during family celebrations. Suddenly, the lights in the room starts to flicker, and in a specific cadence. You might respond and say hello. They flicker even brighter and faster! This is your family member saying hello and letting you know they are around. Instead of freaking out and getting scared, just send love from your heart and let them know you are grateful they are watching over you. It is that simple.

Remember that there is a world beyond this world; we strive to understand and comply with physical, mental, and spiritual laws of nature. Spirit communication between this world and the spirit world by means of mediumship is to bring forth healing, guidance, upliftment, and reassurance. Mental mediumship is pictures, using all of the clairs—your life experiences, visions, symbols, visions, associations, and feelings.

Physical mediumship is messages of smells, sensations in body, touch, sudden change in temperature in the room, rapping, tapping, table tipping, apportation, automatic writing, and trance mediumship. Physical mediumship is when spirit is working with energy frequency and vibration, versus the medium working with these elements.

We get caught up in the phenomena instead of the philosophy behind this. The philosophy is that there is no death, and continuity of life exists for all of us. Here is a list of demonstrations of physical mediumship, but I can't stress enough, to remember the philosophy. Spirit works with energy for the following:

Partial or full human appearances
Direct Voice Communication
Automatic Writing
Telekinesis/Psychokenesis
Channeling Through the Medium
Sounds and Lights
Table Tipping

Transfiguration
Apportations
Ectoplasm (today is very rare)
Levitation
Fragrances and Odors
Rapping and Tapping

Again, this is not to provoke fear. It is spirit working with energy. Love is at the highest vibration, so you don't want to have any fear around this. People come to me for readings, but most of my gifts are with physical mediumship. When I was a child, I worked with spirit and they did so many of these demonstrations to me and for me. It came very easily. In fact, many of these are still utilized by spirit through me, and it is stronger than my mental mediumship. It's about trusting spirit and energy. Just like with mental mediumship, physical mediumship can be developed with practice. It is about setting your intention, and not forcing but allowing spirits to work with energy and you being the conduit.

Partial or Full Human Appearances

Some spirits have been caught on camera physically manifesting. One time when I was getting ready to go on a trip overseas, I was a little apprehensive. While sleeping, I was awakened by the bed shaking because a spirit was walking through my bed, as he looked like he was glowing. He appeared as a hologram, and he stood in the middle of my bed. As he was walking, I heard my mother's voice and she said, "He is a friend of your grandfather's." This man had on a suit from the 1930s, a little tattered as he seemed like he had travelled a great deal, and he had a briefcase in his hand. He said, "My name was Edward, and I will be going with you to ensure your safety." Then he walked through my mattress again and went out the bedroom door. This is an example of a physical appearance by spirit. It was not in my head like mental mediumship, but physically standing in the middle of my bed. At first, I was a little afraid as the bed was shaking as he walked through my bed, but I immediately calmed down when I heard my mother's voice. I trust my mother implicitly. If she hadn't spoken, I might have sent him away without listening to his message. But always send the spirit love, as they come through with a message.

Ectoplasm

Spirits will utilize the etheric energy-matter from the medium's body. This energy is known as ectoplasm. It looks like a white milky, smoky substance. Spirit can manipulate the energy of the ectoplasm, so the physical phenomena occurs. Ectoplasm can be created by spirit in many different forms, visible and invisible, white, or colored. Spirit guides make the decision on what to do with this substance. Once created, the ectoplasm generally emerges from the medium through some body orifice, either the nose or mouth, or through a psychic center located at the solar plexus. Ectoplasm can be used to move objects, for transfiguration, and for physical manifestation of other spirits. The ectoplasm is "collected" by spirit helpers and they manipulate the energy and vibration to create ectoplasm, which they then use in physical phenomena structures, whether it is used for materializations, movement of objects, or physical raps and taps.

Transfiguration

Transfiguration is when there is a sudden change in the someone's appearance. With transfiguration, the face of a spirit person forms over the medium's face or other recipients' faces. You can see this by using a red light. The face can be very clear at times, with the medium's face completely disappearing. Features like facial hair, beards and mustaches, glasses or earrings, smoking pipes or hats are recognized. The hair can change shape and the body shape can change, as well. People in development circles can see the ectoplasm forming on the faces of people sitting opposite of them.

Direct Voice

Direct voice is another type of physical mediumship, where the voice of a spirit speaks to the recipient out of thin air. This happens outside the body, and not in the mental state like clairaudience. In the 1800s and early 1900s, trumpets were used by mediums, where they would use a speaking trumpet sitting on the floor of a circle or table. The trumpet is very much like a telephone to the spirit world. When someone places a telephone call to you, you have no problem recognizing who is calling because you recognize his or her voice. When one listens to the voices that come from the trumpet, each spirit has their own unique voice. The voice of the spirit sounds identical, no matter which of the mediums is leading the group. The trumpet is placed in the center of the circle of people present, and when the atmosphere is right, spirit will speak through the trumpet. The voices are created from an artificial voice box formed from ectoplasm, again taken from the physical medium. Psychic power needs to be generated from the recipients to help form ectoplasm for the communication to take place. Music can be played, or even sing-a-longs help bring raise the vibration and energy. Once the power is sufficient, it can take a few minutes for a spirit to master the voice box. Once the voices come through, they are as clear and powerful as anyone talking in the room. Spirits of men, women, children—people of all ages, languages, and accents can speak. Direct voice mediumship requires complete darkness to function, but again it offers direct proof of life after death as questions and answers can be made to the spirit individuals.

Apportation

Apports occur in a psychic circle or around the home, where a physical object is materialized by spirit guides, to the group of people sitting in circle, or just you personally. Usually this involves a physical object that has been vanished from one location and transported to another, where it rematerializes. It has been known for objects to appear to individuals who are not in a circle and have nothing to do with mediumship or any contact with psychics. The objects can be almost anything from flowers, books, jewelry and even money (usually small-denomination coins, but financial wealth is not important to spirit). Apports can just randomly happen during a psychic circle or at home. Also, objects can appear if you are distraught about losing something. Spirit can also do an apport to try to get your attention, as there might be an important message forthcoming.

Automatic Writing

Automatic writing is another form of physical mediumship that involves letting go of your conscious mind or thought processes in order to write a message from Spirit.

Before you begin automatic writing, the first thing is to set your intention and clear a pathway to allow spirit to guide your hand. Find a quiet place, either in front of the computer or with a journal and a pen, still your mind, and invite your guides into the space where you are sitting. Connect with the paper, your writing hand, and your solar plexus, and allow it to flow. The first few sessions, you might just scribble. Hold the pen lightly in your hand. With practice, spirit will come in and start to write messages.

In any practice of physical mediumship, connect with spirit out through the crown of your head, and draw energy in and send it out from your heart and solar plexus. Become spirit and blend with spirit. Allow the information to flow. Spirit can also take over writing, not putting thoughts into your head, but writing and making the pen move, as you write. You can also receive words, three words at a time. Write them down.

To begin writing, perhaps start with: "Dear Spirit Guides, I wish to connect with you…." You can then ask a question, or you can simply launch in from there. Once you have asked your question or connected, start writing whatever comes into your mind without putting too much thought into it. Trust in the rhythm that flows and tap into the creative juices that live inside, so you can type or write without thought or judgment about what is coming through. The minute you start judging the words that flow, the connection will stop, and you will find it difficult to receive guidance.

Keep writing until your fingers or hand starts firing on all cylinders and you are completely lost in what you are writing. Allow your hands or fingers to be taken over by your guides, and surrender to whatever messages flow. There is a deep feeling of connection that comes through automatic writing. It is a positive feeling that will uplift you and will help you feel connected to your guides.

Telekinesis

Telekenesis is different from apportation. Telekinesis is when an object is physically moved across the table or across the room, whereas in apportation, the object disappears and reappears somewhere else. In telekinesis, you can watch it being moved physically. Another example of telekinesis is spoon bending to show the change and movement of an object. Flowers are used for this demonstration, as well, as flowers respond and are moved easily by spirits.

Levitation of Objects

Levitation is the movement of objects without normal means of support. This can be done by either psychokinetic energy (telekinesis) or using ectoplasm. One of the most amazing examples of levitation was through the mediumship of D.D. Hume. On over 100 occasions during the 1860s and into the late 1870s, he was levitated up to the ceiling and often around the room above the heads of the recipients. I have never witnessed levitation, but like any physical mediumship, it must be practiced and takes years to master.

Table Tipping

In a physical circle spirit creates ectoplasmic rods under the table and it is used to move objects such as a table. I have seen the table move in many ways with people lightly touching the table, so light that you can see fingertips gently touching the surface. The medium is the significant source of ectoplasm, but some regular recipients are used as extra energy resources. In table tipping, you sing songs to raise the vibration in the room and ask yes or no questions—one tap is yes, two taps for no, for example. You must raise the vibration, and the table will start to keep the beat of the song. I have seen tables levitate off the floor and tip in my lap without the legs touching the floor. In addition, I've heard reports of incidents where the table went up in the air, came down, and broke in two pieces. When the table starts moving, there is a lot of laughter and fun for all the participants. You can tell when the energy drops, and it is done. But during the table tipping, it is a lot of fun for everyone!

Raps or Knocks

A very common phenomenon is table raps or knocks. The sounds of these raps and taps can range from soft fingertip taps, to large knocks like knuckles on a table. I've even had situations they kept snapping my water bottle, many times. Quite often you also hear a sound like wood splintering or cracking. On other occasions, ectoplasmic rods can cause raps to occur. With all of these raps or knocks, you can establish a code for yes or no answers to questions. Just like table tipping, you can use one rap for "yes" and two raps for "no." It is quite an effective form of communication, and if you ask the right question, it can also be very informative. I have even had prophetic questions answered, with the answer verified weeks or months later.

Spirit Lights

If the people in a circle are very harmonious it can create conditions for some wonderful phenomena. One of these is the appearance of spirit lights. Spirit lights come in all intensities and colors. Common colors are blue, white, and red, even pink. The colors are seen as bright spots from time to time; however, they can have incredibly intense brightness on rare occasions. The lights are a representation of a spirit's presence and their vibration. The brighter the spirit light usually indicates higher levels of spirit development.

Trance Channeling

In recent years, several mediums have called themselves "trance" channels, when in fact, they were not working in a genuine trance condition. This has been a source of great confusion for many people.

When spirit links with a medium, the spirit communicator has various degrees of control, or overshadows the consciousness of the medium. There must be great trust between the medium and the spirit communicator. The control of the spirit depends upon the intent of communication, as well as the ability of the medium to lend himself or herself to be overshadowed or controlled. This requires a great deal of trust. I have witnessed people who close their eyes and immediately start talking. True channeling of information takes a moment for the spirit to step in and blend energies for the trance to occur. My aunt would channel her guide, Sally. She would take a moment and leave her body as her guide, Sally came in to provide messages. You could ask Sally any question. She would hold this trance state for a long time. When my aunt came back into her body, she didn't recall the session, or what was said, as her identity was not in the body, but Sally took over to deliver messages. The consciousness of the medium steps out, and the medium's consciousness is then open for spirit to communicate.

Trance is considered the strongest degree of spirit control. Yet, even here, there are various degrees of trance control, from light trance to very deep trance. Deep trance is used primarily in physical mediumship.

Genuine trance is a strong sharing of mental and physical energies and consciousness between the medium and the spirit communicator. Physically, there is a slowing of the heart rate, and a slow, deep breathing pattern. There is no rapid eye movement, or REM. If you see someone is having REM during channeling, rest assured they are not channeling spirit. There is a lowering of body temperature, and various degrees of unconsciousness; the eyes can be open or closed. Furthermore, because the spirit communicator is speaking directly through the consciousness of the medium, rather than the medium relating what is being mentally given to them, the voice pattern, inflection, and general manner of speech differ from those normally exhibited by the medium.

Often, there is a broken speech pattern, a reversal of sentence structure, and an overall change in grammar usage. This is very evident in the Edgar Cayce readings, the Seth material, in the book *Seth Speaks*, and in Eileen Garrett's trance communications.

Rarity of Physical Mediumship

Physical mediumship was very common during the last century up until around the 1930s, but it declined rapidly in the 1950s. In the early half of the 20th century, the power and range of phenomena seen was amazing. Unfortunately, these days it is quite rare to see it. People are just not dedicated enough to sacrifice their time and effort into developing physical mediumship. It really does take total selfless devotion to harness and develop this form of mediumship. With all the demands of the information age, and the fast pace of life, we don't slow down to dedicate ourselves to learn physical mediumship. In those early years of the 20th century, a development circle was a social event. Most of the great pioneer mediums began by sitting in a home circle. Nowadays, it is hard to find a development circle for physical mediumship, or any type of mediumship development. We may be on the verge of a new growth in mediumship development circles. Hopefully some of these may turn into physical mediumship development circles. I noticed that during the end of the 1990s, there seemed to be a resurgence of interest in physical mediumship, but it still tends to be an underground movement with closed circles, whose members will sit for years to get the phenomena and do not want any publicity. I can understand this, as I have been with my aunt, where she has served and hosted physical mediumship circles for many years, and although they were not closed groups, it is hard to find the time to dedicate time for development.

Modern spiritual phenomena started appearing in the Victorian period; it was relatively new, and people of course wanted to see it live. They needed evidence of spirit's presence, and of course spirit guides were quite willing to provide evidence of physical manifestations. When people began to accept the continuity of life and mediums' evidence, the masses yearned for more spiritual teaching and philosophy. This gradually reduced the occurrence of physical mediumship. As a counterbalance to physical mediumship, mental mediumship began to be the predominant method. It is my opinion that mental mediumship demonstrates that life continues and there is no death. The need of humanity is to see evidence through "thoughts," has dictated how spirit responded to those needs. Spirit responded by just helping us with mental mediumship, as we started to create new realities with thoughts and feelings, working with universal and spiritual law. I would love to see a resurgence of physical mediumship, but not as a circus act or as a focus on phenomena. I would like to preserve the philosophy of the continuity of life.

Physical Mediumship vs. Mental Mediumship

Physical mediumship can be a lengthy process to develop, sometimes tedious, with no materializations happening in the circle for years. It requires great commitment on everyone's part, and our focus is now short lived, as we are pulled in so many directions. If one or two people have similar types of energies or vibrations, with the other people sitting contributing also to the energies and their own development, it could happen quicker. It may take a while for materialization, but you will certainly have raps, table movement, psychic smells, spirit lights, transfiguration, and other noteworthy physical phenomena, with continued practice.

CHAPTER 9

Final Thoughts

*W*hen doing any type of mediumship, we are working with energy, frequency, and vibration. Always remember that love is the highest vibration in the universe. Love is nonjudgmental, and when we truly love, we can fully trust and accept the flow of things. We work to become harmonious with our surroundings, with a sense of peace. Always keep an open mind, and connect with joy, peace, and your creativity.

You will find additional resources on mediumship and other materials on my website at www.rachellegehman.com. You will find my blog and podcasts on topics that will help develop your mediumship, and ways to work with spiritual and universal law. My goal is to provide the best resources on mediumship, as well as tools to integrate the spiritual world with the physical world.

It is about living from your highest and best self, continually to study and read books on philosophy, and psychology. It is also about being accountable for your behavior, providing readings with the highest level of ethics.

To take your mediumship to the next level, it's not about just providing evidence and delivering messages, but it is connecting with the sweetness of spirit, and allowing the essence of your being to help deliver messages to your recipients with your special uniqueness that makes the time together a wonderful experience for your clients.

Reading List and Additional Resources

Guided
Reclaiming the Intuitive Voice of Your Soul
Author: Hans Christian King

The Magic Mala
A Story that Changes Lives
Author: Bob Olson

Source Code Meditation
Hacking Evolution Through Higher Brain Activation
Author: Dr. Michael Cotton

The Book of Secret Wisdom
The Prophetic Record of Human Destiny and Evolution
Author: Zinovia Dushkova

Through a Medium's Eyes
About Life, Love, Mediumship and the Spirit World
Rev. B. Anne Gehman Volume 1
Author: Ruth Schilling

READING LIST AND ADDITIONAL RESOURCES

In Tune with the Infinite
Author: Ralph Waldo Trine

The Unobstructed Universe
Across the Unknown
Author: Steward Edward White

The Teachings of Silver Birch
Author: A. W. Austen

Self Empowerment
Nine Things the 19th Century Can Teach Us
About living in the 21st
Author: B. Anne Gehman and Ellen Ratner

The Priest and the Medium
The Amazing True Story of B. Anne Gehman and Her Husband
Former Jesuit Priest, Dr. Wayne Knoll, Ph. D.
Author: Suzanne Giesemann

There Is A Purpose: The Story of Anne Gehman, Psychic Spiritualist
Authors: Jerry McCarty and Debra Quarles

You Can Communicate with the Unseen World
Author: Harold Sherman

Miracle Workers: America's Psychic Consultants Adventures in the Psychic
Author Jess Stern

Wisdom in the Workplace
On The Job Training for the Soul
Author: Ellen Krupack Raineri

The Soul's Remembrance
Earth is not our Home
Author: Roy Mills

The Key
A True Encounter
Author: Whitley Strieber

Additional Resources:

Rachelle Gehman
Psychic Medium/Spiritual Counselor
www.solefocused.com
www.rachellegehman.com
Author website: www.theheartfeltmedium.com
Contact: theheartfeltmedium@gmail.com

Lily Dale Assembly
Lily Dale, NY 14752
Phone number: 716-595-8721
https://www.lilydaleassembly.org/

Arthur Findlay College
Stansted, UK
www.arthurfindlaycollege.org
Phone number: 00 44 127 987 3636

Morris Pratt Institute
http://www.morrispratt.org/
11811 Watertown Plank Road
Milwaukee, WI 53226-3342
phone: (414)774-2994
fax: (414)774-2964
info@morrispratt.org

Reference Material

Code of Conduct and The Law

These laws have been passed in the UK and there are other laws in the New Consumer Protection Regulations on Fraud. Please make sure that you are aware of this, as you must not be ignorant of the law. I have copied the UK's law of the Fraudulent Mediums Act 2008. This will help with the expectation of the conduct under laws written to protect recipients, as they should be. There are so many charlatans that have not done the work or have not completed their training. Please make sure you read this and always operate at the highest level of ethics. Under the consumer protection law, here are the sections of the law that is followed in the US, 18 U.S. Code CHAPTER 47— FRAUD AND FALSE STATEMENTS.

Following the second repeal of the 'Fraudulent Mediums Act' in June 2008, also now embodied in Consumer Protection Law. You are at liberty, after a reasonable time, to decide to withdraw your consent to a private reading, should this be the case, any fee that may have been exchanged between us, will be refunded in full. As a general guideline, this should be decided within the first 10 minutes—by either of us.

The Consumer Protection from Unfair Trading Regulations 2008

SCHEDULE 1 Commercial practices which are in all circumstances considered unfair

1. Claiming to be a signatory to a code of conduct when the trader is not.

2. Displaying a trust mark, quality mark or equivalent without having obtained the necessary authorisation.

3. Claiming that a code of conduct has an endorsement from a public or other body which it does not have.

4. Claiming that a trader (including his commercial practices) or a product has been approved, endorsed or authorised by a public or private body when the trader, the commercial practices or the product have not or making such a claim without complying with the terms of the approval, endorsement or authorisation.

5. Making an invitation to purchase products at a specified price without disclosing the existence of any reasonable grounds the trader may have for believing that he will not be able to offer for supply, or to procure another trader to supply, those products or equivalent products at that price for a period that is, and in quantities that are, reasonable having regard to the product, the scale of advertising of the product and the price offered (bait advertising).

6. Making an invitation to purchase products at a specified price and then—
    (a) refusing to show the advertised item to consumers,
    (b) refusing to take orders for it or deliver it within a reasonable time, or
    (c) demonstrating a defective sample of it, with the intention of promoting a different product (bait and switch).

7. Falsely stating that a product will only be available for a very limited time, or that it will only be available on particular terms for a very limited time, in order to elicit an immediate decision and deprive consumers of sufficient opportunity or time to make an informed choice.

8. Undertaking to provide after-sales service to consumers with whom the trader has communicated prior to a transaction in a language which is not an official language of the EEA State where the trader is located and then making such service available only in another language without clearly disclosing this to the consumer before the consumer is committed to the transaction.

9. Stating or otherwise creating the impression that a product can legally be sold when it cannot.

10. Presenting rights given to consumers in law as a distinctive feature of the trader's offer.

11. Using editorial content in the media to promote a product where a trader has paid for the promotion without making that clear in the content or by images or sounds clearly identifiable by the consumer (advertorial).

12. Making a materially inaccurate claim concerning the nature and extent of the risk to the personal security of the consumer or his family if the consumer does not purchase the product.

13. Promoting a product similar to a product made by a particular manufacturer in such a manner as deliberately to mislead the consumer into believing that the product is made by that same manufacturer when it is not.

14. Establishing, operating or promoting a pyramid promotional scheme where a consumer gives consideration for the opportunity to receive compensation that is derived primarily from the introduction of other consumers into the scheme rather than from the sale or consumption of products.

15. Claiming that the trader is about to cease trading or move premises when he is not.

16. Claiming that products are able to facilitate winning in games of chance.

17. Falsely claiming that a product is able to cure illnesses, dysfunction or malformations.

18. Passing on materially inaccurate information on market conditions or on the possibility of finding the product with the intention of inducing the consumer to acquire the product at conditions less favourable than normal market conditions.

19. Claiming in a commercial practice to offer a competition or prize promotion without awarding the prizes described or a reasonable equivalent.

20. Describing a product as 'gratis', 'free', 'without charge' or similar if the consumer has to pay anything other than the unavoidable cost of responding to the commercial practice and collecting or paying for delivery of the item.

21. Including in marketing material an invoice or similar document seeking payment which gives the consumer the impression that he has already ordered the marketed product when he has not.

22. Falsely claiming or creating the impression that the trader is not acting for purposes relating to his trade, business, craft or profession, or falsely representing oneself as a consumer.

23. Creating the false impression that after-sales service in relation to a product is available in an EEA State other than the one in which the product is sold.

24. Creating the impression that the consumer cannot leave the premises until a contract is formed.

25. Conducting personal visits to the consumer's home ignoring the consumer's request to leave or not to return, except in circumstances and to the extent justified to enforce a contractual obligation.

26. Making persistent and unwanted solicitations by telephone, fax, e-mail or other remote media except in circumstances and to the extent justified to enforce a contractual obligation.

27. Requiring a consumer who wishes to claim on an insurance policy to produce documents which could not reasonably be

considered relevant as to whether the claim was valid, or failing systematically to respond to pertinent correspondence, in order to dissuade a consumer from exercising his contractual rights.

28. Including in an advertisement a direct exhortation to children to buy advertised products or persuade their parents or other adults to buy advertised products for them.

29. Demanding immediate or deferred payment for or the return or safekeeping of products supplied by the trader, but not solicited by the consumer, except where the product is a substitute supplied in accordance with regulation 19(7) of the Consumer Protection (Distance Selling) Regulations 2000 (inertia selling) (1).

30. Explicitly informing a consumer that if he does not buy the product or service, the trader's job or livelihood will be in jeopardy.

31. Creating the false impression that the consumer has already won, will win, or will on doing a particular act win, a prize or other equivalent benefit, when in fact either—

    (a) there is no prize or other equivalent benefit, or

    (b) taking any action in relation to claiming the prize or other equivalent benefit is subject to the consumer paying money or incurring a cost.